Why
CELEBRATE
EASTER

OTHER BOOKS BY STEVE RUSSO

Why CELEBRATE EASTER

STEVE RUSSO

BROADMAN
&HOLMAN
PUBLISHERS

NASHVILLE, TENNESSEE

0-8054-2424-5

Published by Broadman & Holman Publishers,
Nashville, Tennessee

Dewey Decimal Classification: 263
Subject Heading: EASTER
Library of Congress Card Catalog Number: 00-063077

Library of Congress Cataloging-in-Publication Data
Russo, Steve, 1953–
    Why celebrate Easter / Steve Russo.
              p. cm.
    Includes bibliographical references.
    ISBN 0-8054-2424-5 (pbk.)
    1. Easter. I. Title.

BV55 .R87   2001
263'.93—dc21   00-063077
                                                         CIP

1 2 3 4 5 6 7 8 9 10 05 04 03 02 01

Contents

Acknowledgments

This book is truly the result of many people working in close cooperation.

Where would I be without all my friends at Broadman & Holman Publishers? They have earned my appreciation for believing in the potential of this project. In particular, I am grateful to Gary Terashita for his initial vision for the project and for being such a great encouragement. I also want to express my thanks to Chip MacGregor for his insightful editing of this manuscript.

Thank you to Dr. Robert Saucy, from Talbot Theological Seminary, for giving the project a review through the eyes of a theologian. I learned much from him as a seminary student and continue to appreciate his gifts and input into my life.

Many thanks to the Russo Team office staff for taking on extra responsibilities so I could concentrate on writing this volume.

My most special thanks, as always, goes to my family. Tami and the kids—Tony, Kati, and Gabi—sacrificed much family time so I could write this book. Their love, patience, and encouragement helped me complete this project.

Ultimately, my hope is that this book will honor the one who is at the heart of this holiday celebration, Jesus Christ. May many people find hope and new life through the Jesus of Easter.

PART 1:

A HISTORICAL PICTURE

CHAPTER 1

The First Easter

Easter is the oldest and most important holiday of the Christian church. It is pivotal to the Christian faith because it commemorates the resurrection of Jesus Christ. Although Easter has been observed in some manner since ancient times, the celebration as we now know it didn't happen overnight. In fact, the idea of pageants, family gatherings, and decorations are relatively recent developments. In the first few years immediately following that first Easter, the holiday wasn't even observed on the same day everywhere. Over the years, as the Easter celebration has become more established, it has been influenced by many people and cultures, including the Jewish Passover and an Anglo-Saxon pagan rite of seasonal regeneration. The result has been a considerable variety of expressions. Yet despite the different Easter traditions that have taken shape, Christians have been consistent about one thing throughout the centuries since that first Good Friday—The resurrection of Jesus is truly something to celebrate!

The best place to begin a study of Easter is in the Bible. Most of the elements of the traditional Christian Easter story have their origin in the first four books of the New Testament. These books give us a detailed account of the death, burial, and resurrection of Jesus Christ.

THE FIRST EASTER

The Gospel of Luke offers some incredible details about the very first Easter. He gives a strong accounting of the last days of Christ, including his arrest and execution. Then, through Luke's careful, historical narration, we acquire the facts about the resurrection of Jesus. We pick up the story in Luke 24.

> But very early on Sunday morning the women came to the tomb, taking the spices they had prepared. They found that the stone covering the entrance had been rolled aside. So they went in, but they couldn't find the body of the Lord Jesus. They were puzzled, trying to think what could have happened to it. Suddenly, two men appeared to them, clothed in dazzling robes. The women were terrified and bowed low before them. Then the men asked, "Why are you looking in a tomb for someone who is alive? He isn't here! He has risen from the dead! Don't you remember what he told you back in Galilee, that the Son of Man must be betrayed into the hands of sinful men and be crucified, and that he would rise again on the third day?"
>
> Then they remembered that he had said this. So they rushed back to tell his eleven disciples—and everyone else—what had happened. The women who went to the tomb were Mary Magdalene, Joanna, Mary the mother of James, and several others. They told the apostles what had happened, but the story sounded like nonsense, so they didn't believe it. However, Peter ran to the tomb to look. Stooping, he peered in and saw the empty linen wrappings, then he went home again, wondering what had happened. (Luke 24:1–12 NLT)

The women came back to the tomb fully expecting to finish the task of preparing Jesus' body for burial. This was a sign of their love and respect for Jesus. The task had been interrupted by the Sabbath—Jesus' body had been hurriedly placed in a tomb before sunset. However, the women were not aware that Nicodemus and Joseph had already finished the burial preparations before placing Jesus in the tomb. According to John 19:39, Nicodemus had purchased one hundred pounds of spices and aloes. He and Joseph had wrapped the body with linen and spices.

In Matthew's Gospel we read that the women were also not aware that there had been an earthquake and that the stone had been rolled away by an angel (see 28:2–4). The Roman guards fainted and then probably took off running when they awoke and saw the empty tomb (Matthew is the only gospel writer to mention the guards). When the women arrived, they found no one around, the stone was rolled away, and the body was gone. (Note: Jesus didn't need the stone rolled away to get out. It had to be moved to let the women and the disciples in.)

While still standing in the tomb, the women were surprised by the appearance of two angels. One angel asked the women why they were looking in a tomb for someone who was alive. Didn't they believe Jesus would come back from the dead as he said he would? The angels reminded the women of Jesus' promises and sent them to find Peter and the disciples and to tell them what had happened. The disciples were skeptical at first but ran to the tomb to see for themselves. Peter was the first one to go inside the tomb, followed by the others. Lying before them were the linen wrappings—ample proof that Jesus was alive. (Even today many people are skeptical when they hear about the resurrection. Like Peter they need time to let it sink in. They also need to see the reality of Jesus' resurrection in the lives of those who are followers of Christ. Ultimately, however, they will only believe after they have finally encountered Jesus for themselves.)

In John 20:11–18 we read how Mary Magdalene returned to the tomb after the others left. As she stood outside weeping, Jesus suddenly appeared to her. It was his first appearance of the day, although several more encounters with other people would follow. For Mary Magdalene and the other followers of Christ, the first Easter was an event of mixed emotions that eventually resulted in unspeakable joy and celebration.

HISTORICAL ROOTS

During the first three centuries after the Resurrection, there was much disagreement between the churches of Alexandria and Rome as to how to calculate the celebration date for Easter. In A.D. 325, the Council of Nicaea—convened by the Roman emperor Constantine the Great—decided that the date should be determined by the Jewish Passover. The council unanimously ruled that the Easter festival should be celebrated on the Sunday closest to the fourteenth of Nisan (the first full moon after or on the vernal equinox). The Council of Nicaea also made the decision that the calendar date of Easter was to be calculated in what was considered to be the chief astronomical center of the world at that time: Alexandria.

Thus, each year the "movable" Easter celebration must occur somewhere between March 22 and April 25. (Eastern Orthodox churches usually celebrate Easter after Western Easter because they follow the Julian rather than the Gregorian calendar.) The entire ecclesiastical Easter cycle runs from Septuagesima Sunday, which may be as early as January, and continues through Whitsun Eve, which sometimes falls in June. This entire cycle can span almost the whole time the earth is spinning from winter to summer.

Traditionally Easter comes at the end of the Lenten Season, which covers a forty-day period beginning on Ash Wednesday and ending on Easter Sunday. It is then followed by forty days leading to Ascension Day. Several other spiritual festivals set their dates in relation to Easter, extending over a long period of time between Septuagesima Sunday (nine Sundays before Easter) and the first Sunday of Advent.

The first title given to the festival—both in the East and West—was "Pascha." This name was used by Europeans for Easter because of the festival's close association with the Jewish Passover. The Spanish *Pascua*, the French *Paques*, the Norwegian *Paaske,* and the Greek *Pascha* all trace their roots back to the Passover.

The origin for the name "Easter" is not certain. Some say the name comes from the German goddess of rebirth, Eostara. In ancient times, the Feast of Eostara was the celebration of the rebirth of Earth. Two symbols for fertility—the Easter bunny and eggs—are carryovers from this feast. The pagan joy in the rising of the spring sun and bonfires parallel the Christian sunrise service and special candles at Eastertime. Other scholars believe the word

Easter comes from an ancient German word *eostarum,* meaning "dawn." In the early church, Easter week was called *hebdomada alba,* meaning "white week," because of the white garments the newly baptized wore at Easter. Later, the plural of "white" was misunderstood as the plural of "dawn," and thus it was translated as *eostarum.*

Many scholars accept the proposal of eighth-century English scholar St. Bede for the origin of the name "Easter." The root is thought to be derived from the Scandinavian *Ostra* and the Teutonic *Ostern* or *Eastre.* This mythical goddess signified spring and fertility. A month corresponding to April was dedicated to her, called *Easturmonath,* and the festival was celebrated on the day of the vernal equinox. Traditions associated with this ancient festival that have survived include the Easter rabbit (symbol of fertility) and colored eggs. Another theory suggests the word comes from *oster,* which means "to rise." Whatever the origin may be for the name "Easter," it is a reference to the east and the rising of the sun. The days on either side of Easter, plus Easter itself, became known as Eastertide.

Easter was observed by early Christians of Jewish origins on the same day as Passover, the fourteenth day of the month of Nisan, the first month of the year. This celebration immediately followed the Passover festival. The date was directed by a Babylonian lunar calendar, and Easter fell on different days of the week from year to year. However, Christians of Gentile origin wanted to celebrate the Resurrection on Sunday, the first day of the week. With their method of dating, Easter always occurred on Sunday, but the date varied from year to year. Historically, Christian churches in the East that were closer to the birthplace of Christianity and had strong old traditions celebrated Easter based on the date of Passover. Those descendants of the Greco-Roman civilization in the West observed Easter on a Sunday.

The church tried unsuccessfully to fix the date of the Easter festival. In 387, France and Egypt celebrated Easter thirty-five days apart. Then around 465, a method of calculation proposed by the astronomer Victorinus was adopted by the church. Pope Hilary had commissioned Victorinus to improve the calendar and assign the date of Easter. Additional significant adjustments were made in the Easter cycle by the Scythian monk Dionysius Exiguus in the sixth century. A bitter dispute regarding the adoption of the changes broke out between Rome and the British and Celtic churches in the seventh century.

Finally, much of the difficulty in establishing the date of Easter was eliminated through the efforts of Pope Gregory XIII in 1582. The Julian calendar was reformed through the adoption of the Gregorian calendar, thus paving the way for an official church calendar. Since the Gregorian calendar was adopted by Great Britain and Ireland in 1752, the entire Western world has celebrated Easter on the same day. However, because the Eastern churches never adopted the Gregorian calendar, their Easter celebration usually falls on a Sunday a week or more after the date observed in the West. Occasionally the dates actually coincide.

Because of all the early confusion and the inaccuracy of the early calendars, we do not know the precise date of the first Easter. It was definitely in the spring, but it could have fallen anytime in late March or April. However, the most important thing to know is that there was an Easter, a time when Jesus Christ died on the cross for our sins and rose again on the third day, conquering death and guaranteeing eternal life for everyone who believes. Knowing the precise date doesn't change what Jesus did for us on the first Easter.

EARLY EASTER CELEBRATIONS

The original Christian celebration of Easter encompassed the death-resurrection-exhalation of Jesus as one commemoration. However, in the fourth century, Christians started celebrating Good Friday separately to commemorate the death of Christ. A procession was staged in Jerusalem from Gethsemane to the Sanctuary of the Cross, followed by special readings. This was the beginning of the Good Friday commemoration, as it is now known. Easter Sunday was then entirely devoted to the observance of the Resurrection. In the early church this included a special time for baptisms and restoration of prodigal sons and daughters who had experienced a change of heart.

A number of other ancient festivals and legends celebrated by people of other faiths were also associated with this time of year. In a Greek legend, the goddess of earth, Persephone, daughter of Demeter, returns to the light of day from the underworld. To the ancient Greeks, her return symbolized the resurrection of life after the barrenness of winter. In similar manner, according to Phrygian belief their all-powerful deity went to sleep at the time of the winter solstice. At the spring equinox, various ceremonies with dancing and singing were performed to wake him up. The early Christians, many of whom were brought up in the Hebrew tradition, considered Easter to be a new highlight of the Passover festival, commemorating the ascension of the Messiah.

The early church struggled with the gods of the pagans and non-Christians. Some of the traditions to honor these gods were tough to break, and many found their way into early Easter customs. Take for example the Easter fire. Spring bonfires to honor the sun god were prohibited until 1752. It was Saint Patrick who established a new tradition with them. While serving as a missionary in Ireland, Patrick recognized that it was difficult for the Irish to give up their spring fire rites. So in place of the old pagan custom, Patrick presented the people with a new Christian fire ceremony. Everyone was brought together on Holy Saturday for a huge bonfire outside of the church. Then the new fire of spring was blessed.

It didn't take long for this new custom to spread across Europe. In a short period of time all Christian churches made it a part of their Easter services. Then a new custom developed from the Easter fire: people would light a stick from the special bonfire at church and bring it home with them to light candlesticks, lamps, and stoves. Over time, Easter fires came to symbolize the conquest of light and life over darkness and the grave.

Another variation on the Easter fire is the Easter candle, which has taken the place of the Easter fire in many churches today. In the early years of the Christian faith, candle ceremonies were an important part of Easter celebrations. People preparing to join the church gathered at the church on Easter Eve. As the sun set in the west, each person pointed in that direction and made a vow to have nothing more to do with the prince of darkness. Then each person turned toward the east, where the sun rises, and pledged to follow Jesus, the "Light of the World." Songs of jubilation then broke out at the sight of the first star. The night shone like day as candles and lamps throughout the town lit up. Even small children stayed up for the "night of light."

THE UNIQUENESS OF EASTER

Easter's importance to the Christian faith makes its commemoration essential. The Resurrection's meaning, though truly a religious one, has also gained acceptance as a celebration of spring, of the life and rebirth of a new season. Thanks to the early church, Easter is an established holiday, a time when we remember a Savior that no other world religion has—God, who became a man to die on the cross for his people and then be raised from the grave to rule forever.

CHAPTER 2

Special Days and Customs at Easter

It would be next to impossible to fully understand the place Easter holds in the lives of secular and religious people without examining the special days, anniversaries, and customs that have been observed down through history during the Easter season. Some of the topics discussed in this chapter have long disappeared from common practice. Others have taken on a new twist in the twenty-first century. Whatever the case may be, looking at these days and traditions not only can add depth to our celebration of Easter, but we can also gain new insight into how much the death and resurrection of Jesus Christ has impacted the history of our world since that very first Easter.

SPECIAL DAYS ON THE CALENDAR

SHROVETIDE

Shrovetide is the carnival season, or "last fling," that precedes Lent. It is actually the English name for the last three or four days before Lent starts. These days include Egg Saturday, Quinquagesima Sunday, Collop Monday, and Shrove Tuesday. Today, in many European countries, this is still considered a season of elevated carnival activity. At a time in history when the Lenten fast was much stricter than it is today, Shrovetide was widely celebrated with wild parties, games, sports, dancing, and bizarre antics. Children went door to door demanding gifts of meat or eggs, pelting the houses with rocks and broken pottery if they were refused. Other young people celebrated by stealing small household items that had not been locked inside, or doorknobs.

Other hugely popular traditions among adults and kids were cock fighting, wrestling matches, throwing competitions, and horse races. It was a time for mischievous pranks and jokes, freedom from rules, and just about anything else imaginable that allowed participants to "let loose" before the solemn and reflective Lenten season began.

Before the time of the Reformation, these last few days were also meant to be spent quietly confessing sins and observing a pious custom called shriven, from which we get the name Shrove. Church bells would ring out to signify the faithful being shriven. After the Reformation, these same bells became known as the Pancake Bells. They signaled the start time for sports games and for pancakes to be made.

In countries that do not have carnivals, Shrove Tuesday primarily suggest pancakes. This special day normally falls in February or within the first few days in March. Some believe our modern-day pancakes are a combination of the small wheat cakes made at the Roman Feast of Ovens and a practice of Christian housewives right before the start of Lent. Before the fast began, all remaining fats and butter had to be disposed of, so pancakes were made. On Collop Monday, eggs, bacon, and fried collops of meat would be eaten for the last time until the end of the fast.

Septuagesima Sunday

This is the ninth Sunday before Easter. On this Sunday, before the start of Lent, the Alleluia (meaning "Praise the Lord") is officially discontinued in Catholic churches to indicate the approach of the somber Lenten season. The Alleluia is not sung again until Easter Sunday. Pope Alexander II instituted this practice in 1060.

Lent (Lenten Season)

The Easter festival is preceded by forty days of Lent and continues for forty days afterward until Ascension Day. Observed since the fourth century, the name comes from the old English word *Lenckten,* which means the spring or "lengthening of days." Lent begins on Ash Wednesday and concludes on the eve of Easter. For the most part Lent was viewed by the early church as forty days of fasting; however, it is more likely that it was initially a fast of only forty hours. This fast was mainly observed by candidates for Easter baptism.

Later, in the seventh century, this forty-day period was universally recognized as a way to honor the fast of Jesus detailed in Matthew 4. Over time this forty-day season also came to commemorate the forty days Moses spent on Mount Sinai, as well as the forty hours Jesus spent in the tomb. Since early times, Lent has also been known as a time for abstinence, charity, and acts of devotion in order to prepare for the Easter celebration. For some Christians, Lent is a time of quietness and contemplation that helps strengthen their faith. A common theme on which pastors focus during Lent is the "Seven Last Words of Christ" spoken on the cross.

In the Eastern Church, Lent covers a seven-week period of time, beginning on a Monday because it excludes both Saturdays and Sundays from the forty-day count. The Western Church observance only lasts six and one-half weeks because only Sundays are excluded. This season is set aside as a period of penance in preparation for the most important festival of the church calendar: Easter.

Some peoples actually view all of Lent as a carnival time. The most well-known carnival celebration at this time of year is New Orleans' Mardi Gras, which marks the final day before the forty days of Lent begin. The term Mardi Gras is French for Fat Tuesday. Even though it refers to a specific day, the term also refers to a longer period of celebrations leading up to Mardi Gras Day. Similar celebrations are held in other cities in Alabama, Florida, and Louisiana.

During the season of Lent some people observe two other celebrations: World Prayer Day and Brotherhood Week.

World Prayer Day. This special day of prayer, which falls on the first Friday in Lent, was first proposed by the Presbyterian Church in the United States in 1887. Other denominations soon joined in to support this prayer vigil by Christians all over the world. Each year a specific theme is selected for the day. The primary sponsor of this event that crosses denominational lines and racial barriers is the National Council of Churches.

Brotherhood Week. This celebration, observed by a huge cross section of religious institutions, originally began on the Sunday closest to Washington's birthday. Gradually it has evolved into a week-long emphasis, with some organizations scheduling programs throughout the entire month of February.

The purpose of Brotherhood Week is to help different religions understand one another and to encourage dialog on various faith-related issues. Sponsored by the National Conference of Christians and Jews, the celebration places special emphasis on youth programs.

ASH WEDNESDAY

The first day of the season of Lent in Christian (Western) churches is Ash Wednesday. The name comes from the practice of putting ashes on the foreheads of people to symbolize their sorrow for sin and death. Pope Gregory I is thought to have introduced the custom in 1091. In the Roman Catholic Church, the custom is practiced by using ashes from burned palm branches or brushwood acquired from the previous year's Palm Sunday observance. These ashes are subsequently blessed before Mass on Ash Wednesday.

During the ceremony, one priest places ashes (in the form of a cross) on the foreheads of the other priests serving in the ceremony as well as members of the congregation. The priest also recites the following over each person as part of the custom: "Remember that you are dust, and to dust you shall return."

MOTHERING SUNDAY

This custom began in England and took place on the fourth Sunday in Lent. On this day, young people who lived away from home were allowed to return to the "mother church" in which they were raised or baptized. They brought with them small gifts to place in front of the altar. Those who returned would also visit their mothers, bringing with them gifts of flowers, cakes, and other small gifts. The returning young people did the chores while those usually in household service were given the day off.

Prior to the Reformation, Mothering Sunday was more of a festival and featured games and feasting, which provided a break from the strictness of Lent. The entire family attended church, then enjoyed a meal of roast lamb or veal followed by "simnel" cakes (from *simila,* the fine wheat flour from which cakes are made). At this afternoon meal, the mother was treated as the "queen of the feast."

After a long period of decline, this special day has taken on new life and has even become rather commercialized, with a variety of shops selling "Mother's gifts." After World War II in many parts of England, Mothering Sunday became known as Mother's Day. This was largely due to the influence of American soldiers stationed there during the war.

LAETARE SUNDAY

Another name for the fourth Sunday of Lent is Laetare, which dates back hundreds of years. While celebrating Mass on this day (which is also mid-Lent), the Pope would carry a golden rose in his hand as a symbol of joy. Starting in the fifteenth century, the single rose became a cluster of roses made out of pure gold and decorated with precious stones. After blessing it, the Pope often confers this priceless bouquet upon churches or dignitaries as a sign of honor.

PASSOVER

This is an important feast in the Jewish calendar. The eight-day celebration commemorates the exodus of the Hebrews from Egypt and their safe retreat across the Red Sea. The name of this important Jewish festival (from the Hebrew word *pesach,* meaning "passing over" or "protection") refers to instructions God gave to Moses in Exodus 12. In order to motivate Pharaoh to allow the Hebrews to leave Egypt, God was going to kill all the firstborn animals and people in the nation. In order to protect themselves, the Hebrews were instructed to mark their dwellings with lamb's blood so that God could identify them. The angel of the Lord then passed over the Hebrew homes and destroyed the firstborn in every Egyptian home.

The Passover celebration begins after sundown on the fourteenth day of Nisan, which is the first month of the Jewish church year. Those Jews living outside the boundaries of ancient Palestine observe the holiday for eight days. On the first two nights they participate in a special meal called the Seder. The meal consists of prescribed foods, each of which symbolizes some aspect of what the Hebrews went through during their Egyptian enslavement. Horseradish (the bitterness of the experience) and chopped nuts and apples in wine (the building mortar used by the slaves in their forced labor) are just two examples. Those Jews living within the boundaries of ancient Palestine observe Passover for only seven days and conduct a Seder one night.

During the entire passover observance Jews must abstain from eating leavened bread, instead substituting *matzo,* an unleavened bread. This symbolizes the unleavened bread eaten by the Jews during their escape from Egypt, when they had no time to prepare raised bread. Tradition also mandates that during Passover all meals be prepared and served using dishes and utensils set aside strictly for this festival.

The story of the exodus from Egypt is recounted and prayers of thanksgiving are offered to God for his protection as part of the Seder.

HOLY WEEK

This last week of Lent is called Holy Week. Beginning with Palm Sunday, the week continues with Maundy Thursday, Good Friday, and Holy Saturday.

The last days in the life of Jesus are celebrated during this week, and significant events that have helped shape the Christian faith are reiterated. Initially this week was to be free from worldly activity and devoted to religious practices, but as time passed, some churches made a switch to holding services only at night during Holy Week and designating Good Friday as the only holy day. Because it commemorates the great deeds of God for the human race, it is sometimes called "Great Week" by Orthodox Christians and Roman Catholics.

PALM SUNDAY

Traditionally this is a day of rejoicing. The Sunday before Easter commemorates the triumphal entry of Jesus into Jerusalem one week before his resurrection. Jesus had come to the city to observe the Hebrew Passover festival of freedom. Each spring, at the first full moon, Jews commemorated the freeing of their ancestors from Egyptian slavery.

The name comes from the palm branches that were laid in the pathway of Jesus by his followers, who acclaimed him king that day. The Palm Sunday custom dates back to the fourth century. Since the Middle Ages, many Western churches have commemorated this day by blessing palm branches and distributing them to people attending Palm Sunday services. The branches are then worn on clothing and kept as a sign of devotion. These palms are thought to bring good luck by some people.

In Wales, the name for this special day is *Sul y Blodau* which means "Flowering Sunday." Traditionally on this day, people adorn the graves of family members with colorful flowers. It is a sort of ritual preparation for Easter, with the dead being able to symbolically share in the resurrection with the living, as signified by the flowers.

MAUNDY THURSDAY

The Thursday before Easter Sunday—also known as Holy Thursday, Green Thursday, or Pure or Clean Thursday—is set aside to observe and commemorate Christ's Last Supper with his disciples, which was held the evening before the Crucifixion. That night Jesus celebrated the Passover feast in the upper room of a friend's home. Jesus provided a pattern for his disciples of a special communion service that they were later to hold in memory of him. He also used the occasion for another symbolic gesture, illustrating the ministry of service by humbling himself and washing the disciples' feet.

The name "Maundy" comes from the Latin word *manda-tum*, which means "commandment" and refers to the new commandment Christ gave at the time he washed the disciples' feet (John 13:5, 14, 34). It is the first word of a song that is sung as part of a special ceremony on that day. In many churches there is an evening service where Holy Communion is served. The Catholic liturgy includes a foot-washing ceremony, or *pedilavium*. During this rite, participants wash the feet of twelve people in remembrance of Christ washing the feet of the disciples. Traditionally, gifts of food, money, and clothes were given to the poor after the foot-washing ceremony.

The name Pure or Clean Thursday originated in a time when people did not have the luxury of bathing as frequently as we do today. People bathed and cleaned themselves in preparation for the Easter celebration.

In some countries the Thursday before Easter is also called Green Thursday. Criminals who were being pardoned wore green or carried pieces of green plants. People believed it was bad luck not to eat green foods, so they consumed green salads, herb soup, and spinach served with eggs. The tradition of eating green foods on Green Thursday is still popular in many parts of Europe.

GOOD FRIDAY

Christians commemorate the anniversary of the death of Christ on the Friday before Easter. Traditionally it has been viewed as the most solemn feast of the year as time is taken to commemorate all that Christ went through on the cross. In English-speaking countries the name is believed to be a corruption of "God's Friday." It is a day set aside for mourning and reflecting.

In parts of Europe it is sometimes called "Great or Holy Friday." In Denmark it is known as *Langfredag* or "Long Friday." In this case the word *long* has a similar meaning to *great*. In northern England, it was often called "Care Friday" because it was a time of grief and passion.

Until the fourth century there was no separate Good Friday observance. Originally it was set aside as a day of fasting in preparation for the all-encompassing Easter celebration of the death, res-urrection, and exaltation of Jesus Christ. A fourth-century proces-sion in Jerusalem staged from Gethsemane to the Sanctuary of the Cross, followed by a series of special readings, was the beginning of the Good Friday observance as it is now known.

Starting in the sixteenth century, Good Friday services took place in the morning. However, in 1955 Pope Pius XII decreed that they be held in the afternoon or evening.

In the Protestant tradition, Good Friday services often focus on the last seven words of Christ and are held between the hours of noon and 3:00 P.M. to commemorate the hours Christ hung on the cross. For the Roman Catholic Church, this is a day of mourning. The traditional Catholic service consists of special readings, a veneration ceremony, and communion. In figurative remembrance of the death of Christ, the altar is stripped and the candles extinguished.

Even for those with little religious inclination, this day was set apart as different from every other day of the year. Some people even fell prey to superstitions, including a reluctance to do cer-tain types of work for fear of possible misfortune. For many years, miners refused to go down in the shafts on Good Friday, think-ing that some disaster would happen if they did. Blacksmiths would not shoe horses or do any of the other work of their trade that involved nails because of the horrible way nails had been used in the Crucifixion. According to an ancient legend, it was unlucky to wash clothes on Good Friday because whoever did would find blood-stained water or clothes spotted with drops of blood.

There are many variations and special ceremonies performed on Good Friday by different denominations and ethnic groups. In parts of Europe, South America, the United Kingdom (and the Commonwealth), and the United States, Good Friday is a legal holiday.

Tre Ore Service. Tre Ore (three hours) is a popular service of devotion that begins at noon on Good Friday and concludes at three o'clock. It was first performed in Lima, Peru, by the Jesuits and quickly spread to Catholic and Protestant churches throughout the world. Often the service centers on the last seven words Jesus spoke on the cross.

Ceremony of Platsenitsis (Winding Sheet). On the afternoon of Good Friday, elders in the Greek Catholic church carry a cloth with a picture of the Lord's dead body painted or embroidered on it. Along with the priest, the elders walk in procession to the shrine of the Sepulcher, where the cloth is placed on a table to be venerated by the people. Once the ceremony is completed, the cloth is placed inside a carved wooden case representing the tomb of Christ.

HOLY SATURDAY

Easter Eve, as it is sometimes called, is a strange interlude in the Easter observances. It commemorates the one day during his ministry that Jesus was not alive and present with the disciples. The mood is quiet yet expectant in towns where Holy Saturday is observed. The mood greatly changes with the first evening stars. Many people keep lights burning all night so the light rays will link with the morning sun. In Spain and Mexico joyful celebrations on Easter Eve include horns honking, whistles blowing, fireworks exploding, and even an occasional cannon booming.

EASTER SUNDAY

The greatest Christian celebration of the year commemorates Christ's victory over death as he triumphantly left the grave. The pageantry of Easter crosses all denominational distinctives so that Protestant churches now vie with Catholic churches in celebrations of richness and grandeur.

THE OCTAVE OF EASTER

The period of time extending from Easter Sunday through the following Sunday is called the Octave of Easter. In ancient times, those who had been newly baptized wore white garments, the liturgical color of Easter, signifying joy, light, and purity.

WEEK OF RENEWAL

The week following Easter is named the Week of Renewal because of the crucial restoration achieved by the resurrection of Jesus Christ. The "critical restoration" is the restoration that took place between a holy God and sinful man. A restored relationship between God and man is made possible by Christ's death on the cross and his resurrection.

ASCENSION

Forty days after Jesus' resurrection from the dead, his post-resurrection appearances came to a conclusion. His earthly mission had been fulfilled. Jesus left the conditions of life on earth behind and resumed his place with the Father. The transition that took place was not one of "going up to heaven," but rather one of going to a different dimension of reality. It was not only a change of place, but a change of state. It was a physical and spiritual transition for him.

THE FEAST OF THE ASCENSION

This feast, viewed by many as another one of the great festivals of Christianity, is celebrated forty days after Easter on Thursday. The theme of this feast is Christ ascending on the clouds toward the outstretched hand of God the Father.

THE FEAST OF PENTECOST

The conclusion of the Easter season occurs ten days after Ascension Day and is called the Feast of Pentecost. This is the day when the apostles reported that the Holy Spirit had entered into them. Christians believe that this is also the day the church began.

SUNDAY

This day of the week is an Easter symbol that is observed all year long. The reason Christians worship on Sunday is because of the connection to the Resurrection.

WHITSUNDAY

Whitsunday is another name for the Christian feast of Pentecost, the day when the Holy Spirit descended on the apostles

(Acts 2:1–4). For the early church it was a traditional time for administering baptism. In the Church of England and other Anglican churches, the festival is called Whitsunday because of the white robes that were traditionally worn by those who had been newly baptized.

DISTINCTIVE CUSTOMS

BLESSING OF THE EASTER FIRE

In some traditions on Easter morning a fire is struck from flint in the churchyard, and from it the new Easter fire is lit. All the lights and candles in the sanctuary are extinguished. A triple taper is lighted, representing the Trinity (Father, Son, and Holy Spirit). It is held high to lead the procession into the dark sanctuary. Then the blessing takes place, followed by the lighting of the Paschal candle and the rest of the lights in the sanctuary.

EASTER CANDLELIGHT

A flame of any size at Easter has come to represent light after darkness and life after death. The Easter candle has taken the place of the Easter fire in many churches today.

EASTER PARADES

The parades that are held after Easter Sunday services are carryovers from long ago and originate from superstition. In ancient times it was believed that if princesses and peasant maidens wore a new garment at Easter, they would have good luck throughout the year. The colorful outfits were a reflection of the broader concept that Easter is a time of new life and a fresh start. The popularity of this custom has been declining over the years, but people still like to pull out their best outfits to make a vivid Easter statement.

EGG GAMES

In ancient Rome, people celebrated the Easter season by running races. The races were run on an oval track and eggs were awarded as prizes.

Easter egg hunts take place in the morning or afternoon of Easter Sunday. Children search inside or outside the house for eggs that the Easter bunny "brought" while they were asleep. Sometimes prizes are rewarded to those who find the most eggs. These hunts may also take place in a park as part of a community-wide celebration. In several countries, including Germany and the United Kingdom, children play a game in which eggs are rolled down a hill or against one another. The person with the egg that remains uncracked the longest wins.

PASSION PLAYS

These plays started in the Middle Ages and dramatize the Easter story. The most famous of all the passion plays dates back to 1634 in southern Germany. Now once every ten years it is presented in Oberammergau. There are also many cities in the United States where they are performed annually.

TENEBRAE (LAS TINIEBLAS)

The word means "darkness." Originally this old ritual was used in Catholic churches, but in recent history it has been adopted by some Protestant churches and is included in Wednesday and Thursday night services. One after another the candles in the church are extinguished, leaving only one lit. This single candle represents Christ and is carried behind the altar after the ceremony. This gradual darkness was supposed to represent the burial of Christ and express grief over Christ's death. After the last prayer has been said in the service, a sign is given and a single lighted candle is brought back out and placed on the altar. The reappearance of this single candle signifies that Jesus' light was not extinguished with death. It also implies the promise of the Resurrection.

THE EASTER VIGIL

In some Catholic churches, an all-night service is held beginning Saturday evening. It begins with two dramatic rituals and leads directly into Easter morning.

STATIONS OF THE CROSS

This homage first came into popular use in the fifteenth century by Western Christians. It is thought to have originated during the time of the Crusades, when Holy Land pilgrims marked off the sites associated with the Lord's journey to the cross in Jerusalem and the surrounding area. Upon returning to their homes in Europe, the travelers created replicas of these stations in their churches. The number of the stations may vary, even though they were "fixed" at fourteen in the eighteenth century. The order of the stations is as follows:

1. Jesus is condemned to death.
2. Jesus is forced to carry his cross.
3. Jesus collapses the first time under the weight of the cross.
4. Jesus sees his suffering mother.
5. Simon helps to carry Jesus' cross.
6. Veronica wipes the face of Jesus.
7. Jesus collapses the second time.
8. Jesus speaks to the women of Jerusalem.
9. Jesus collapses the third time.
10. Jesus is stripped of his clothes.
11. Jesus is nailed to the cross.
12. Jesus dies on the cross.
13. Jesus' body is removed from the cross.
14. Jesus' body is placed in the tomb.

The content of these stations has never been determined by any official church authority because the custom has always been viewed as an act of personal devotion.

SUNRISE SERVICES

Ancient civilizations held spring festivals long before there was an Easter Sunday. They worshiped a variety of gods and celebrated the return of spring by dancing and singing around huge bonfires. Some people even leaped through the flames and offered sacrifices to celebrate the victory of spring over winter. Of supreme importance among the gods of ancient people was the sun god. It was the sun god who sent rays of light over fields for crops to grow. Early Christians drew a parallel between the sun and Jesus. Just as the sun died each evening and came back to life each morning, so Jesus died and rose again.

The custom of going to a lakeshore, a park, or a hilltop before dawn on Easter morning has grown more popular over the years. Multitudes gather in the darkness with great expectation as they watch the eastern sky for the first glimmer of light. To some it is a deeply moving religious experience, while for others it is a way to express hope for a better life.

A FINAL THOUGHT

It is my hope that after having read this chapter you have gained new insight into how the Easter season has impacted previous generations. Reviewing these days and customs can help us refocus our thoughts and emotions as we prepare for Easter, enabling us to have a more meaningful celebration. I also recommend, where appropriate, the adoption of some of the customs and special days into your own observance of the Easter season. Whatever you do, however, make sure you keep focused on what the death and resurrection of Jesus Christ means to you and your family.

CHAPTER 3

Easter around the World

In what country is it bad luck not to eat green salad on Maundy Thursday? What is a favorite food served at Easter in Poland? How do people celebrate the holiday in Italy? Where can you find friendly elves at Easter? Few people are aware of the various ways Easter is observed around the world. From the tiniest villages to megacities, in the deserts and in the jungles, there is an Easter celebration. However, sometimes the form taken is rather remarkable!

In many places around the world, Easter is a time of celebrations, bonfires, parades, and pilgrimages. There are also many unique traditions and customs practiced at Easter time in different countries. And, as you will see, there are some fascinating legends that people have followed in the past and in some cases observe today.

The following section is by no means exhaustive, but it will give you a better idea of just how different Easter celebrations are in various parts of the world. Get ready for Easter around the world!

EASTER IN ALBANIA

Eastern Orthodox Christians in this country observe Good Friday and Easter later than Protestant and Roman Catholic churches. The celebration is delayed to comply with the ancient decree of the Council of Nicaea, which declared Easter should not be celebrated until the observance of the Jewish Passover is finished. This decree has been widely adhered to by Eastern churches, though not by Western ones.

EASTER IN ARMENIA

People gather in a churchyard three days prior to Easter to break eggs. The object of the game is to strike another person's egg (being held stationary) with the point of your egg. If your egg cracks, you turn it over and try again. If your egg cracks on that end as well, you lose it to your opponent. Once you lose an egg, you must produce another one and continue this process. The person with the strongest egg will win the most eggs. The cracked eggs that have been won are then sold at a reduced price.

According to Armenian tradition, the sun dances on Easter morning; it's the only time all year that this occurs. Because watchers cannot look directly into the sun, they look into mirrors in order to see the sun dance. There is rarely an Easter morning that the weather is not clear.

EASTER IN AUSTRIA

A special custom with pretzels dates back many centuries in this European country. As part of the Palm Sunday observance, pretzels are hung on palm branches.

The custom of gently tapping someone with a green branch, or the "stroke of health," at Easter time is believed to bring that person health and good fortune.

Many people still enjoy an old custom that uses wooden hand clappers to strike the hours instead of using bells. Beginning with Holy Thursday evening, young men walk through the town with their clappers, singing old Easter carols. A stanza of one of these songs goes like this:

We beg you, people, hear and hark!
It's nine o'clock, and fully dark.

EASTER IN BELGIUM

The priest in Walloonia distributes unconsecrated wafers to children to sell to families. The proceeds are given to needy families in the community. The wafers are then nailed over the front door of each home to protect that family from evil.

EASTER IN CANADA

Some French Canadians still believe in ancient Easter water customs. Many still bathe with water that has received the traditional Easter blessing. They believe the water has the power to cure illness, and often keep small bottles of the water to use throughout the year.

EASTER IN THE CZECH REPUBLIC

An ancient custom that has now become ceremonial is the switching of women for eggs. With a willow whip, a man performs a traditional whipping of the women to get colorful eggs in return from them. Gently whipping women at Easter recalls the flogging of Christ. As part of the old Roman festival of Lupercalia, women were scourged to assure fertility. Historically, the egg was widely known as a symbol for fertility.

Young people also had a variation of this tradition that they practiced on Easter morning. Armed with a whip made of braided willow branches, each young man visited the home of a girl in the village. The goal was to get there before she got up in order to whip her from bed. Once again, this was symbolic of the flogging Jesus received before he was crucified. Generally, the young girl was prepared to placate the visiting young man with gifts before she received too many blows. The gifts were Easter eggs that each girl had carefully decorated. The eggs were colored deep purple with white designs of flowers or birds—purple represented the holiness of the Lenten season, while white was symbolic of the blessed Easter day. Other possible gifts included an embroidered handkerchief or an embroidered shirt if the young man was her fiancé.

On Easter Monday, the girls went to the boys' homes and whipped them out of bed, seeking gifts in return. Since only women decorated eggs, the boys gave gifts of candy, brightly colored skirts, or fruit.

At Easter time people enjoy eating a special coffee bread called *babovka*.

EASTER IN DENMARK

It is a tradition to climb Frederikburg Hill in Copenhagen at dawn on Whitsunday (Easter Sunday) to observe the sunrise and see the sun "dance."

EASTER IN ENGLAND

Another name for Palm Sunday is "Spanish Sunday." The name comes from an old children's custom of making a sweet drink by shaking up small pieces of Spanish licorice in a bottle of water. However, ordinary water cannot be used in the making of this drink. Only holy water, obtained through a special excursion to a well or another source in the neighborhood, may be used. This tradition has no real connection to the Christian observance of Palm Sunday. It may be a leftover practice from the days of ancient well worship.

Up until the end of the nineteenth century, people believed that by breaking pottery on Good Friday, the jagged edges of each piece would penetrate the body of the betrayer, Judas Iscariot. There was also a custom of dragging a straw figure called a "Jack-a-Lent" through village streets on Ash Wednesday. This figure was supposed to personify Judas Iscariot. It would be pelted with mud and stones, then finally "executed" by being shot or burned.

EASTER IN FINLAND

Strong oral tradition tells of old charms and incantations used to cure injuries or invoke blessings. Charms were oftentimes used by householders to rid their homes of unfriendly elves. At Easter time when the elves appeared, they could be frightened away by calling out:

Hyi, hyi, Hytola
The dogs of Hytola bark.
My little girl, my little boy,
Look at them coming from afar.

However, not all elves were unfriendly or unwanted at Easter time. Tradition says that on Easter Sunday friendly household elves who lived in the barn used to visit the house to wish the master and mistress good fortune. Carrying branches of pussy willow with which they gently struck the couple, the elves cried out:

Switch, switch.

Be fresh and healthy,

Be well for the coming year.

As many twigs,

So many calves.

As many branches,

So many colts.

As many catkins,

So many lambkins.

EASTER IN GERMANY

On Grundonnerstag (Green Thursday or Maundy Thursday) green salads are traditionally served. According to tradition, eating something green will protect your health. An old German superstition held that someone who refused to eat green salad would turn into a donkey. Among the Pennsylvania Dutch the day is known as *Green Dunnestag*.

German tradition also says that the *antlassei* or Holy Thursday egg is supposed to stay fresh all year long.

There is an old Bavarian custom of burning the "Easter Man" on Holy Saturday. A rough straw figure is nailed to a cross and set on fire with the "new fire" brought from the church. Popular belief at the time said that with the Easter Man's destruction so goes sickness, hunger, personal adversity, and the dangers of bad weather. The ashes were then collected on Easter Monday and dispersed over farmlands in keeping with the belief that this would make them more fertile.

EASTER IN GREECE

A favorite family food at Easter time is a round flat loaf of bread decorated with Easter eggs and inscribed with a cross. This is very similar to a special bread from a Portuguese custom.

EASTER IN ITALY

On Holy Saturday in Florence, crowds gather around oxcarts loaded with fireworks standing next to churches. Without notice, a dove-shaped firecracker flies out of the church window on a wire and lands in the oxcart. The fireworks explode and send the dove back up the wire and into the church. If the dove reaches the altar before exploding, shouts of joy ring out and everybody anticipates good luck in the future. The explosions of light and sound are expressions of joy and are another way of saying there is new life and hope at Easter.

Italians bake a special pizza bread with eggs for their Easter celebration.

EASTER IN IRAQ

Christians decorate their homes at Easter with beautiful flowers. A favorite flower to use is wild tulips they call "lilies of the field."

EASTER IN JORDAN

Families look forward to having special honey pastries for the Easter holiday. A similar traditional pastry is served in Syria at this time of year as well.

EASTER IN MEXICO

Families gather armloads of colorful tropical flowers and bring them to their church to be blessed by the priest.

In Taxco, a huge reed tower approximately one hundred feet tall is constructed just to hold the Easter fireworks, which explode in domino fashion from one to another. Those gathered around to watch then enjoy the brilliant exploding colors as they form shapes of animals, birds, flowers, and crosses in the night sky.

EASTER IN THE PHILIPPINES

A beautiful Catholic folk tradition that dates back hundreds of years is the blessing of the young coconut palms on Palm Sunday, or *Domingo de Ra*. For the most part, the traditional ceremony is a children's activity and is based on the songs "Pueri Habraeorum," which are sung as the palms are disbursed:

The Hebrew children bearing branches of olive,
Went forth to meet the Lord crying out
And saying: Hosanna in the highest!

The Hebrew children spread their garments along the way,
And cried out saying: Hosanna to the Son of David,
Blessed is He who comes in the name of the Lord.

The immature white palm branches are cut from trees on the Saturday before Palm Sunday by young boys. The branches are then woven into a variety of elaborate designs including flowers, birds, and crosses. Each young boy is then expected to carry a palm branch to church on Easter.

Young girls between the ages of six and twelve spend Saturday afternoon gathering flowers and getting their white dresses ready to wear the next day. On Easter Sunday the young girls ("the Angels") stand on platforms, *bahay-bahayan,* in the churchyard and shower people with flowers after Mass. The little "Angels" also sing "Hosanna" while on the platforms. Each young boy attempts to catch one of the flowers. The priest then gives his blessing to everyone there and sends them home to prepare for Holy Week.

Young boys proudly display their palm branches all the way home. Then dad and mom congratulate them for participating in such a treasured custom. The children may receive gifts of new clothes or toys as a reward. The palm branches and flowers are then carefully stored away.

EASTER IN POLAND

On Holy Saturday evening, people take a basket of food to the church to be blessed after the midnight Easter service. The baskets include: eggs because they are a symbol of life (Christ came from the tomb alive); rye and babka bread (Jesus was the bread of life); ham or kielbasa sausage which signifies the God-man Jesus; horseradish representing the anguish Christ went through on the cross, and a lamb made out of butter or sugar (decorated with the Polish flag) depicting Jesus—the Lamb of God—who takes away the sins of the world. A favorite food to eat is *baba*, a cakelike bread in the shape of an old peasant woman's full skirts.

The day after Easter in Poland (*Dyngus* or Easter Monday) is a boisterous water day for children. Splash Monday, as it is often called, derives from an old Polish practice. On this day children armed with sprinkling cans and pails of water (both scented and plain) lie in wait for gullible victims, some of whom will receive a gentle sprinkling while others will get a drenching. The origins of this custom are unknown. One theory connects it to the need for and difficulties surrounding individual and communal baptisms at Easter time.

EASTER IN PORTUGAL

The Portuguese enjoy eating a round flat loaf of bread decorated with Easter eggs and inscribed with a cross. This is much like a special bread that is traditionally served in Greece.

On Good Friday, people living in the country burn a wooden or straw image of Judas Iscariot. Before being burned, the figure is cursed, kicked, and beaten. Sometimes it is also hanged amid the cheers of the crowds who gather to watch.

EASTER IN SWEDEN

Firecrackers are used in a rather interesting rite by children at Easter. Pictures of witches are drawn by Swedish children. They write Easter greetings on each picture. The children then dress up like witches and put these special Easter letters in the mailboxes of their friends. Then firecrackers are set off in the street. The witch pictures represent evil spirits, and the noise of the firecrackers is supposed to frighten them away.

EASTER IN SYRIA

A favorite Easter holiday food among children and adults is a special honey pastry. Something similar is enjoyed in Jordan during this same time of year.

EASTER IN THE UNITED STATES

CALIFORNIA

A thirteenth-century custom—The Blessing of the Animals—is celebrated by Hispanics on Holy Saturday. Dogs, cats, pigeons, parakeets, chickens, horses, donkeys, and even turtles are brought to the church to receive God's blessing. This is most likely a reworking of an ancient Roman custom that called for blessing animals in order to encourage their fertility. This rite usually took place in early April when tribute was paid to Venus, the goddess of love.

On this same day, some Catholic Hispanics also practice the custom of burning a likeness of Judas Iscariot, the one who betrayed Jesus.

LOUISIANA

The Journal of American Folklore lists the following Creole Good Friday beliefs:

- There is always rain on this day because even the heavens weep on the day of the death of Christ.
- If you go fishing, fish will always bite on Good Friday.
- An egg laid on Good Friday will turn to wax if kept until the next Good Friday.
- If you dig in the ground, you will see blood. (Some interpret this to mean you will cut yourself; others think it means the earth is actually bleeding.)
- Never dig in the ground to plant flowers; you will see blood before nightfall if you do.
- Someone is always hurt at Good Friday picnics.
- Roosters always crow at three o'clock in the afternoon on Good Friday.
- If you plant parsley on Good Friday, it will not go to seed.

- The blood of *Bon Dieu*—Jesus Christ—will run out in the rows if you cut open the ground on Good Friday.

MARYLAND

Memoirs of the American Folklore Society records the following folklore about hatching eggs in Maryland:

- If you set a hen on Good Friday, you will have all kinds of speckled chickens.
- Every egg will be hatched if you set a hen on Good Friday.

NEW YORK

According to *The New York Folklore Quarterly,* cabbage should be planted on Good Friday before the sun rises or it will form a club root and grow up in a straight stalk. This is also the best day for planting radishes, lettuce, tomatoes, and sweet peas.

NORTH CAROLINA

The *Journal of American Folklore* reports that Good Friday is a chosen day for planting everything, especially beans. Fridays are good days for planting things that hang down, like beans and grapes, because Friday is "hangman's day."

PENNSYLVANIA

The Pennsylvania Dutch have some interesting Good Friday health cure beliefs, according to *Pennsylvania Folklife:*

- Whooping cough. If you take off a child's clothes and place him in the wheat, and then put the wheat in the mill the very same day, the child will not get whooping cough.
- Warts. If you have warts, get up early on Good Friday morning and get a potato. Don't speak to anyone, go out to the barn, and cut the potato in two. Rub the potato over the wart and then feed the potato to a cow. The warts will go off you and onto the cow.
- Rupture. If you have a rupture, get a soft-shelled egg that was laid on Good Friday. Take off the skin of the egg, put it over your rupture, and name the three greatest names: Father, Son, and Holy Ghost, and the rupture will go away.

WASHINGTON, D.C.

Every year the President and First Lady host a White House Easter egg roll on the south lawn. Tens of thousands of children and their parents attend this annual event. Children compete in a variety of games involving rolling eggs on the lawn. The American Egg Council usually donates several thousand real eggs, and the White House contributes thousands of wooden ones to be given away as prizes and souvenirs.

EASTER IN THE UKRAINE

For many generations Ukrainians have adorned Easter eggs. The decorating has grown into such a well-respected art that a woman who is especially gifted is called a *pysarka*. Often she is asked to decorate special eggs for people in nearby villages. The eggs to be decorated are not cooked because the raw shell absorbs the color much better. The egg is held with a soft tissue during the decoration process so that the oil from the hand does not keep the dye from being absorbed. The egg is left in the shell because a blown eggshell is too fragile. The inside of the raw egg eventually dries to the shell, making it stronger. After the design is finished, the egg is varnished, giving this special decoration a life span of many years. These attractive eggs, or pysanky, are then given to friends and relatives on Easter morning with a special greeting, *"Krystos voskres"* (Christ is risen). Those receiving this special gift reply with, *"Voistynu voskres"* (He is risen indeed!)

EASTER IN YOUR WORLD

This is only a sampling of ways Easter is celebrated throughout the world. It might be fun to add some of these ethnic observances to your family's holiday celebration. You must remember, however, that no matter what you do, always keep Christ as the main focus of your celebration. He is the one who conquered death, and he enables us to experience the hope of Easter 365 days a year.

CHAPTER 4

Easter Eggs, Bunnies, and Jelly Beans

Easter is a season and a day filled with vivid images and symbols: jelly beans, baby chicks, white lilies, new clothes, brightly colored eggs, and chocolate bunnies. All of these have come to represent Easter, just as pumpkins and black cats have for Halloween or reindeer and candy canes have for Christmas.

Weeks before Easter Sunday, the stores begin displaying a host of items, all representing various aspects of this colorful spring celebration. You can find everything from Resurrection ties and eggs to baskets filled with candy and stuffed animals. Easter ranks fourth on the list of top occasions to send greeting cards in the United States. Hallmark sells an estimated 120 million greeting cards at Easter (Christmas, 2.6 billion; Valentine's Day, 900 million; and Mother's Day, 150 million).

Candy seems to be the biggest seller at Easter time. According to the International Mass Retail Association, among adults celebrating Easter, 67.4 percent plan on buying candy. They will spend an estimated $1.5 billion on chocolate bunnies (34 percent), jelly beans (28 percent), malted eggs (9 percent), creme-filled eggs (8 percent), marshmallow animals (5 percent), and miscellaneous other candies (14 percent). Two percent aren't sure what they will buy.

Easter symbols vary from one city or country to another, yet each symbol means essentially the same thing. All date back hundreds or even thousands of years. Some have roots in early Christian church celebrations, while others originate in pagan customs. Let's take a look at some of the popular foods, decorations, and symbols that we have come to associate with Easter time. Many you will immediately recognize, while others will not be quite as familiar to you.

ANIMALS AND FOODS

BUTTERFLY
Its entire life seems to be symbolic of Easter. In the beginning the caterpillar stands for life, and then the cocoon represents death. Finally a butterfly emerges—as if by magic—from the cocoon, signifying the Resurrection.

CHICKENS
The chicken is a symbol of new life just like the egg, which is a chicken-to-be. Baby chicks, whether stuffed or alive, are always popular at Easter.

DONKEY
The Castilian donkey has very unusual patches of dark hair. One runs the length of his back while another crosses his shoulder. Legend says that because this was the animal on which Jesus chose to ride when he made his stately entry into Jerusalem, the donkey will always bear this cross.

DOVE
Referred to in the Gospel accounts at the time Jesus was baptized, the dove is best known as the symbol for the Holy Spirit.

EAGLE
In ancient times it was thought that the eagle restored its life after flying so close to the sun that its feathers became scorched. The eagle is the only bird known to be able to look directly into the sun without harm.

EASTER BUNNY

It is hard to pinpoint exactly where or when the Easter bunny became part of the celebration, but almost anywhere that Easter is celebrated, there is an Easter bunny. The Easter rabbit has connections to a time when people worshiped the sun and moon. The white rabbit is a symbol of spring fertility (because of their ability to produce many young), and it supposedly brought gifts of brightly colored eggs to children who had been good.

As an Easter symbol, the bunny's origins can be traced to German writings from the 1500s. The first edible Easter bunnies appeared in the early 1800s and were made of pastry and sugar. German immigrants who settled in the Pennsylvania Dutch country introduced the Easter bunny to American folklore during the 1700s. Next to a visit from *Christ-Kindel* (Santa Claus) on Christmas Eve, a child's greatest delight was the appearance of *Oschter Haws* (Easter Bunny) on Easter morning. Legend taught that if children were good, the *Oschter Haws* would lay a nest of colored eggs for them.

Initially children would build a nest in the garden, barn, or even an isolated spot in the house. The nests were made from the bonnets of the girls and the caps of the boys. Eventually, as the tradition of the Easter bunny spread across the country, fancy Easter baskets took the place of the bonnets and the caps.

The Easter bunny tradition varies from country to country. In Panama, a painted rabbit called the *conejo* brings eggs to children. In German-speaking countries and Switzerland, children wait for the Easter hare or *Oster Haas*. This hare is bigger and faster than a rabbit, with longer ears and feet. Sometimes children make nests of leaves or grass or even special little gardens for the hare.

The Easter rabbit or hare has been accepted throughout history as another symbol of new life. Because it is also thought to be weak and dependent on the kindness of others, the rabbit has traditionally been seen as a symbol for man, who places his faith and trust in Christ.

Eggs

Eggs were fascinating and mysterious to early man. The ancient Persians, Egyptians, Phoenicians, and Hindus all believed that the earth was hatched from one huge cosmic egg. According to legend in the Samoan Islands, the great god of the people, Tangaloa-Langi, was hatched from an egg. To ancient Druids, serpent eggs were sacred. People in the early world saw the egg as a miracle—new life emerged from something that resembled a stone. The egg was adopted by early Christians because of its relationship between the renewal of life and Easter.

Colored eggs originated in an ancient Anglo-Saxon festival for the goddess of spring and fertility: Teutonic. The eggs were painted bright colors to represent the sunlight of spring and were used in egg-rolling contests or given as gifts. The custom of giving eggs as gifts during spring festivals to celebrate new life was also practiced by the ancient Chinese, Greeks, and Persians. Today, when a new baby is born to a Chinese family, a bright red egg is sent to relatives and friends in place of an announcement card.

Winters in northern Europe were harsh during the Middle Ages, and food became scarce by spring. Giving up meat and eggs during Lent was not only a religious observance but also a practical way of stretching food supplies. So a fresh egg at Easter time was precious. Castle servants usually received an egg from royalty as a gift at Easter. Children who were hungry would roam the streets at Easter, begging for eggs. Even today in some European villages, children go from house to house asking for Easter eggs. This tradition is similar to kids going trick-or-treating at Halloween in the United States.

Throughout ancient history, people came to believe that Easter eggs had magical powers. People in Yugoslavia, Bulgaria, and Greece used to think that burying painted eggs in the ground at Easter would make grapevines grow well. The British thought that the yolk of an egg laid on Good Friday and kept for a hundred years would turn into a diamond.

Centuries ago, people living in eastern Europe turned decorating Easter eggs into an art form. People living in the country made their own dye for eggs. Onion skins or hickory was boiled to make the color yellow. Light red came from madder root. To get brown, coffee or walnut shells were used. Wrapping the eggs in leaves and ferns before boiling created a pattern on the shell. Women were the primary egg decorators and would begin working weeks in advance on egg designs. No two eggs would be alike because of the variety of designs—crisscrossed lines, dot patterns, plant and animal shapes, and even the sun. Once finished, the eggs were blessed at church and given to special friends and relatives as gifts.

And where there are Easter celebrations and eggs, there are games and contests. Some games involve rolling eggs down a slope or toward a hole in the ground. Other games call for the eggs to be tossed high in the air or rolled into each other like marbles. Even though the egg games do not reflect the deeper meaning of Easter, they are another avenue to express the joy of the holiday.

Throughout ancient history eggs were a symbol for life. The origins of the Easter egg are unclear; no one really knows for sure where the idea came from and how it traveled to the Western world. Easter eggs were first mentioned in a book written more than five hundred years ago. However, long before that a Christian tribe in North Africa had a custom of coloring eggs at Easter. One thing we know for sure, the Easter egg custom started a long time ago.

FISH
The fish symbol was initially used by early Christians as a code to avoid arrest and persecution. The letters found inside the fish symbol are Greek. They are the first letters of the five Greek words meaning: Jesus Christ, Son of God, Savior.

LAMB
The symbolism of lambs at Easter originated in the Jewish Passover, when God spared the Hebrew homes marked with the blood of a lamb (see chap. 2, "Passover"). The lamb took on a different meaning as Jewish tradition began to blend with Christian customs. The lamb was a sacrifice to God for the Hebrews, and the life of Jesus was the sacrifice for Christians. Thus the lamb became

an Easter lamb—a symbol of Jesus' death for us. Jesus is referred to as the Lamb of God and also the Good Shepherd.

The Easter lamb also has a broader and more secular meaning. Early farmers and shepherds believed that it was good luck to meet a lamb during the Easter season. Tradition said that if you looked out your window on Easter Sunday and saw a lamb, you could expect even better luck. This was especially true if the lamb's nose was pointing toward your house. It was also believed that a lamb or a dove were the only two forms the devil could not take.

For centuries roast lamb has been a popular Easter dinner. In countries like Italy and other nations in the East, lamb is still the preferred meat for Easter.

LENTEN AND EASTER FOODS

Food is always a special part of any celebration. We have already mentioned a few foods that are commonly associated with Easter. The tradition of eating lamb at Easter time has connections to the Paschal lamb that was roasted and eaten at Passover. Also it is not unusual to find centerpiece figures of lambs made out of butter, sugar, or pastry. Then there is the custom of eating as many eggs as possible. Whether in special dishes or just hard-boiled, eggs have become a staple of Easter time.

We could fill several volumes listing all the favorite foods and recipes for Easter celebrations that people eat in different parts of the world. However, there are three that have special historical significance that are important to mention.

Fromajadas. Fromajadas is another name for cheesecake. An ancient Minorcan custom of street singing on Easter Eve is at the heart of this tradition. Groups of young men, accompanied by guitar and violin, roamed the streets of St. Augustine, singing a hymn of praise beneath people's windows. The words of the hymn go like this:

> Ended are the days of sadness
> Grief gives way to singing
> We come with joy and gladness
> Our gifts to Mary bring.

The boys would approach a home they wished to favor with their song or from which they hoped to gain a favor. They knocked quietly on the window or shutter. If they heard a knock from within, it meant their visit was welcome. They would begin singing. If they heard no response from within, they would move on to another house. They would follow the hymn of praise with a verse asking for the accustomed gifts:

The owner of this house
Ought to give us a token,
Either a cake or a tart
We like anything
So say you not no.

The window was then opened, and if they sang well, cakes or other pastry were dropped into a bag carried by one of the boys. The gifts were acknowledged with the boys singing:

The owner of this house
Is a polite gentleman.

If no gifts were given, the boys then sang:

The owner of this house
Is not a polite gentleman.

These bands of boys were kept busy singing throughout the town until midnight. They hoped to acquire the most favored cake, one made out of cheese. Consequently, the song they sang from house to house became known as the cheesecake song, or *Fromajadas*.

Hot-Cross Buns. Hot-cross buns are a customary Easter food with pagan origins. Part of the Anglo-Saxons' celebration to welcome spring included consuming small cakes. Early Roman missionaries decided it was best to try and incorporate the cakes into the Easter celebration in some way rather than eliminate them from the customs of new converts. The compromise included drawing a cross on the cakes and blessing them. According to one account, a monk living in England baked hot-cross buns six hundred years ago and distributed them to the poor at Easter time. No one knows for sure if that was the beginning of the tradition or if he was carrying on a custom that had started earlier.

No matter how this tradition actually got started, it's a delicious custom that many enjoy. Bakers in England used to stay at their ovens all night long baking buns for families in the town. Vendors then carried trays of buns through the streets shouting:

Hot cross-buns, hot cross-buns,
One a penny, two a penny, hot cross-buns;
Smoking hot, piping hot,
Just come out of the baker's shop;
One a penny poke, two a penny tongs,
Three a penny fire-shovel, hot cross-buns!

Over time, various beliefs developed about the magical powers of hot-cross buns. These included: eating the buns on Good Friday so your home would be safe from fire all year long; putting the buns back in the oven to harden, then grating the hardened buns to take as medicine in water or milk; or hanging them from the ceiling to bring good luck to the house or protection against lightning. Farmers used them to keep rats out of their cornfields, and sailors took them on voyages to avoid shipwrecks.

These cakes have withstood the test of time and appear in bakeries and stores today around Ash Wednesday. Most are only available at Easter time. They are spicy buns with raisins inside and shiny brown tops with a white icing cross on top.

Pretzels. Pretzels were made by early Christians in the Roman Empire at Easter time. They were made from a special dough of only flour, water, and salt because fat, eggs, and milk were prohibited during Lent. The dough was shaped like two arms crossed in prayer to remind people that the Lenten season was a time of contrition and devotion. Originally these little breads were called *bracalle,* or "Little Arms." The Germans later came up with the term *brezel* or *prezel* from the original Latin word, giving us our word, pretzel.

Pretzels have become a hugely popular food and are consumed throughout the year. Next time you enjoy one, look carefully and see if you can spot a person with his arms folded. In many parts of Europe, pretzels remain a Lenten food, making their annual appearance on Ash Wednesday.

LION

In ancient times, people believed that lion cubs were born dead. Then when they were three days old, the father lion would breathe into them and bring them back to life. They believed this symbolized Jesus lying dead for three days in the grave and then coming back to life.

OWL

These birds prefer darkness to light. Long ago people held to the legend that an owl was a symbol of people always in the dark, in need of a savior.

PEACOCK

In ancient history the peacock was an Easter symbol. It sheds its beautiful fan of blue and green feathers each year. Then every spring it becomes a new bird with a brilliant array of colorful new feathers. To early Christians the peacock was a symbol of new life emerging from the old—a resurrection.

PHOENIX

According to legend, the phoenix was an awesome bird, similar to an eagle, yet adorned with red and gold feathers. It was said to live for five hundred years. Frequently this mythical bird would fling itself on a funeral blaze and be consumed in the flames. It would then rise from its own ashes and start life all over again. People thought this symbolized death and resurrection. In ancient Egypt, the phoenix was a symbol of the sun, which seemed to die each night and rise again with the dawn.

SWALLOW

An ancient legend says that on the day Jesus was crucified, a little bird flew by and called out to him, "Cheer up! cheer up!" Since that time this small bird has been known as the "bird of consolation," or swallow.

WHALES

Throughout the ages, many people have viewed the Old Testament story of Jonah as a prophecy. Jonah lay in the belly of a great fish for three days and was then spit up onto dry land. This parallels Jesus being in the tomb for three days before finally emerging into the daylight.

COLORS AND DECORATIONS

BELLS

The sound of church bells ringing on Easter Sunday signifies that the fasting and mourning are over. In many European countries, bells on churches and other buildings are silent from Holy Thursday until Easter Sunday. Farm people in the Middle Ages were troubled when the bells were silent. In order to bring some comfort to their families, parents would say, "The bells have flown to Rome, but they'll come back for Easter." Even to this day, small children living in central Europe are told that the church bells have gone to visit one of the holy tombs or to visit the pope in Rome. In France, children believe church bells fly to Rome and locate Easter eggs for those who have been good during the year.

In some eastern European countries, an ancient custom is still observed by people. Beginning on Easter morning, bells ring continually until night, with short pauses in between, as a reminder that Easter is the greatest holiday of all.

CANDLES

A variety of candles are burned in Easter celebrations. They are especially important in the vigil and midnight services that occur before Easter Sunday. Jesus is called the "Light of the World," thus the close association with the light of candles. On Good Friday, many churches extinguish their candles to symbolically represent Jesus' light temporarily going out.

COLORS

The colors that are most frequently used in Easter decorations are essentially the same ones associated with springtime. Whether vibrant or soft, these colors represent newness and vitality.

- Green: nature and hope of eternal life. Ancient people took hope as green began to appear on bare branches in spring. In some countries the Thursday before Easter is also called "Green Thursday." Priests during the Middle Ages wore green robes on this day.
- Purple: royalty and mourning. Purple decorates the altar and adorns statues during Holy Week. In the ancient world, purple dye came from a specific shellfish in the Mediterranean Sea. Because each fish could only give a small speck of color, only the wealthy could afford it. Purple became the mark of royalty.
- White: purity, light, and joy. It can be seen in Easter candles and lilies.
- Yellow: sunlight, radiance, and royalty. It is also the color for April, the month in which Easter is most frequently celebrated.

PASCHAL CANDLE

The body of Christ and the return of light to the world through his resurrection are personified by this candle. A cross is cut in the wax of this large candle. At the top is the Greek letter *alpha* and underneath it the Greek letter *omega*. In the four angles of the cross are carved the numbers of the coming year.

CLOTHES, FLOWERS, AND PLANTS

CLOTHING

People throughout the ages have looked forward to shedding their heavy winter garments for lighter ones in the spring. Easter is a traditional time to bring out new and colorful clothes. After attending church, many people still enjoy a walk in the park to enjoy the warmer weather and to "show off" their new outfits. In fact, Easter parades like the one held in New York City attract thousands of people each year. Onlookers watch for celebrities and gaze at the traditional and the not-so-traditional garb of those in the parade. The custom of "parading" actually has deep significance that dates back a long way.

For two or three hundred years after the resurrection of Christ, it was traditional to baptize new believers the week before Easter. Because of the new white robes they wore after their baptism, Holy Week was often called "White Week." As time passed, the early church grew in size and Easter became a much more significant holiday. Attitudes changed and by the Middle Ages people were expected to dress in fresh clothing at Easter, even if they hadn't been recently baptized. People generally took off their heavy winter clothes—sometimes many layers—for the first time in months on "Pure Thursday" of Holy Week. If they were fortunate, they then put on something new after bathing in cold rivers and ponds. The less fortunate simply put on a freshly washed set of old clothes.

After attending church on Easter Sunday, it was time for the traditional special walk through town and into the fields. Families dressed in their spry Easter clothes would stop at certain spots to sing special Easter hymns and to pray. Often someone at the head of these "mini-parades" carried a lighted candle.

These customary Easter walks lost their religious significance over time. Nevertheless, people continued to enjoy dressing up and taking walks as part of the Easter celebration. Superstitions developed over the years regarding Easter clothes. For example, it was considered bad luck to not wear something new. Therefore, no matter how poor you were, you would always try to have something new to wear, even if it was only a new shoestring or hair ribbon.

People applied the same idea of the "newness" of spring to their homes and traditionally did a major cleaning before Easter. The fireplace was cleaned, the hearth was swept, and fresh flowers were placed on the clean stones. Hence the origin of our traditional "spring cleaning."

FLOWERS

Whatever flower or plant someone uses at Easter for a decoration represents all species of flowers and plants. Everything green that is growing out of the ground signifies new life and hope for the future.

EASTER CACTUS

A popular spring-blooming cactus found in the northern hemisphere, it has flat stems and bright red blossoms that become visible about Easter time.

LILY

Although the lily is one of the most popular and symbolic flowers at Easter time, it is not even a spring flower. This waxy white flower has its origins on some islands near Japan. The lily made its way to America via Bermuda many years ago. Growers have now learned how to make it bloom in time for Easter. Over time lilies and other flowers that grow from bulbs became symbols of life after death. The bulb signifies Jesus tomb; the blossom, the Resurrection.

The large white blossoms are a reminder to Christians of the new life that is available as a result of the resurrection of Jesus Christ.

NARCISSUS

This springtime flower of white or yellow blossoms, which grows in the Alps, has been an Easter flower for hundreds of years. However, before it was part of the Christian Easter celebration it belonged to a Greek myth about spring and the changing seasons.

As the myth goes, the goddess Persephone was picking flowers in a meadow one day when all at once dozens of narcissi bloomed from a plant at her feet. As she bent down to pick them, the earth split open and she saw Pluto, the god of the underworld, in his black chariot. From that time on Persephone was forced to live in the underworld with Pluto for six months out of every year. Her mother, Demeter, would grieve for Persephone while she was underground during winter. When Persephone returned to the world, she brought springtime with her.

Ancient pagans believed there were magical powers in the plants and trees that turned green in the spring. Good luck and health were brought to anyone who was touched by a leafy green bough. The custom of gently tapping someone with a green branch, or the "rod of life," was also said to bring that person health and good fortune. As people became Christians, they brought with them many of these springtime customs and made them Easter traditions. Over the course of time it became hard to remember a day when these customs were not originally Christian.

ELEMENTS AND SYMBOLS

WATER

The custom of drenching someone with water on Easter Monday dates back to pagan days. Children and adults alike enjoyed splashing water on one another. Not only was this custom fun, it was supposed to bring good luck and health. People believed that both plants and water had special magical powers. One of the ways this "amazing" power was demonstrated each year occurred when the winter's solid ice on lakes and rivers turned back to water in the spring. People believed this springtime water had the capability of making them strong and powerful. Right after the ice melted each spring, individuals took a bath in the water and sprinkled it on all their farm animals.

The early church disliked these strongly pagan water customs. But rather than eliminate them altogether, priests made them "Christian" by blessing all water—lakes, streams, and ponds—in the neighborhood at Easter time. People then began saving small amounts of water collected at Easter because of its distinctive healing power. They would also delay taking their spring baths until after the water had been blessed.

Today, "splashing" is still a popular Easter season tradition. Young girls are touted with silly rhymes and doused with water by young men. Children dress up in costumes and visit farms. The farmer's wife is treated to a special rhyme of the season and splashed with a bit of water. In turn the farmer's wife gives the children gifts of eggs or candy.

In some parts of Europe this splashing custom has been modernized. Instead of using water, people bring good luck wishes for the coming year with a squirt of perfume. Water is not as identifiable as other more common Easter symbols like bunnies, lilies, and eggs; however, it remains an important ancient symbol of the holiday.

CHI-RHO

This is the oldest monogram for Jesus Christ. It is formed by placing the first two letters in the Greek word for Christ, *X (chi)* and *P (rho),* together.

CROSS AND CRUCIFIX

A cross signifies the death of Jesus Christ for all mankind. There are many styles of crosses used in the Easter celebration by people of different faiths. More than fifty forms of the cross are found in Christian art. In medieval times, most large churches were built in the shape of a Latin or Greek cross as a symbol of Christ's body.

A crucifix is a cross with a small figure of Jesus' body hanging on it. This represents the sacrifice Christ made by dying on the cross. The empty cross, without the body of Christ, is a reminder of Christ's victory over death and the hope of eternal life.

To many early Christians, these creatures, foods, colors, and symbols were a vivid representation of Jesus. Each item added to the celebration and festivity of this all-important holiday.

The same is true for us today. Whether it's new clothes, brightly colored eggs, or a waxy white lily, the many symbols of Easter all say the same thing in a little different way: Easter is the awakening of life and a time of hope. What are some of your favorite symbols and foods? There may be some new ones you have just read about that you want to adopt into your family's commemoration of Easter. Whatever symbols you choose to incorporate, remember that each one should help to enhance your observance of Easter, not detract from it. Easter is about more than bunnies and jelly beans; it's about new life that can only be found in the one who conquered death—Jesus.

WHAT'S A CHRISTIAN TO DO WITH THE EASTER BUNNY?

There will come a time in the life of every parent when he or she will have to decide what to do with the Easter bunny. For most it will come much sooner than later, especially if you have younger children. What is the right thing to do with this soft, cuddly animal with long ears that appears to deliver baskets of goodies and colorful eggs on Easter? Must we choose between Jesus and the Easter bunny, or are there other options?

There's always advice readily available when it comes to cultural issues like the Easter bunny. I was being interviewed on a radio talk show in Pittsburgh, Pennsylvania, regarding my book *Halloween: What's a Christian to Do?* when Joyce called the show. "I don't have anything to do with something unless it's in the Bible," she said.

I replied, "Joyce, do you drive a car? Do you use a telephone or electricity in your home? These things aren't mentioned in the Bible. I appreciate your zeal to want to remain biblically focused, but that reasoning is not only faulty, it's also not what God is trying to communicate to us in his Word about life in the twenty-first century."

There's an excellent principle from the Bible that should serve as our foundation for the decision-making process regarding the Easter bunny. Paul writes in 1 Corinthians 10:31: "So whether you eat or drink or whatever you do, do it all for the glory of God." God must permeate our lives so that we do all for his glory. We must always keep questioning ourselves, "Is what we are doing glorifying God?"

So what are our options when it comes to the big rabbit and Easter? First, we can simply not participate in anything at all associated with the Easter bunny. This is certainly a valid option, but it presents a problem that will need to be dealt with if you have younger children. The Easter bunny is a very big part of the Easter season in our culture. Kids will want to know why they can't do what their relatives, friends at school, and others in the neighborhood are doing with the Easter bunny. And how come they didn't receive a basket from the Easter bunny filled with candy and colorful eggs? This is definitely not an insurmountable problem. However, is it possible to allow our children to have the Easter bunny as part of their holiday tradition and not miss out on the real reason for celebrating Easter? I think it is.

First, let's remember it's extremely difficult to make the connection between the modern-day Easter bunny and ancient pagan rituals. Secondly, before we get too carried away about holiday traditions, let's remember all the things that are such an integral part of our culture, things like birthday cakes and even calendars and the days of the week—all of which have pagan roots. Make sure you are looking at the big picture and being consistent in the process. Choose your battles carefully.

Our main concern must be keeping what Jesus accomplished through his death and resurrection as the main focus of Easter and not letting any holiday traditions, including the Easter bunny, diminish the reason for our celebration. It's not necessary to deprive your children of good fiction so long as they understand the difference between fact and fiction. If you are careful and wise in how you incorporate the Easter bunny tradition, it can be fun for you and your children and also provide a great springboard for your family's discussion about why we celebrate Easter.

Also, be careful about being so opposed to a tradition with which you disagree. You may lose sight of what Easter is all about. Sometimes I think Christians are so busy telling everyone what we are *against* that we forget to tell them what we are *for*. In this case, make sure you are more passionate about sharing the truth of Easter than you are about sharing what you think is wrong with it.

Let's keep our celebration of Easter creative, fun, and joyful. But most of all, let's honor God in the process. Without "Christ in you, the hope of glory" (Col. 1:27), we wouldn't have Easter.

PART 2:

EASTER TAKES ON CULTURE

CHAPTER 5

The Great Easter Debate

Christianity, from its earliest days, has communicated the belief that more than two thousand years ago an itinerant preacher from Palestine got into trouble with civil authorities and was executed in a humiliating way, only to be raised from the grave three days later. And because Jesus rose from the grave bodily, those who believe in him will live eternally and also have a new body.

Skeptics have continually said this is impossible. Many liberal Christian theologians believe that after his death, Jesus lived on only in a spiritual form, without a physical presence. In the anthology *The Resurrection*, published by Oxford University Press, several secular university philosophers apply tools of modern logical analysis to support a belief in Christ's bodily resurrection. This anthology is a result of the 1996 "Resurrection Summit" at the New York Catholic Archdiocese Seminary, where eighteen papers were presented.

Reverend Reginald Fuller, Professor Emeritus at Virginia Theological Seminary, writes that Jesus' Easter restoration was not as a visible, bodily being. He believes that later on in church history, Christians developed the "materializing" of the risen Christ. William P. Alston, of Syracuse University, rebuts Fuller by concluding that in spite of the possibility of some New Testament material being made up later, it's reasonable to believe that there were bodily appearances of Jesus of the general sort that are recorded in the Gospels.

Then there is Stephen T. Davis' essay, which asks the question, "Did the original witnesses to the risen Christ see his body as a material object through normal eyesight, or did they have a subjective vision with no body present?" Ultimately, Davis rejects the subjective approach by citing that Jesus was not just seen by people who believed he had risen. Davis refers to "Doubting Thomas" from John 20. He also thinks the strongest argument is the physical detail in the Gospel accounts. The first four books of the New Testament say that Jesus showed his hands, feet, and side, and he walked, spoke, ate, was touched, and distributed food.

If the average person listens to too much of this "outside" philosophy, it's easy to become confused. However, sometimes one can become just as confused listening to what is being said *inside* churches today. In many cases the desire to be culturally relevant and "seeker sensitive" causes the message of the Resurrection to be reduced to a mere vague and passing thought. There has been a de-emphasizing of the importance of what the Bible actually teaches concerning the resurrection of Jesus Christ. This breeds ignorance, which can be dangerous to spiritual health and well-being.

In contrast, the early church dwelt on the Resurrection constantly. It was the central focus of every speaker in the Book of Acts. The message "He is risen" radically changed an apathetic generation of the Roman Empire. It turned them upside down and inside out. This radical generation then went out to communicate this message to the world. It is a message so powerful and so unique that it needs to be shared more than once a year at Easter.

Considering the fact that the resurrection of Christ is the single most important event in history and that it has profound implications for our lives, it's imperative that we settle the great debate for ourselves. Did Jesus really rise from the dead? And if so, then how does the Resurrection affect our daily lives? Let's examine what the Bible teaches about the first Easter Sunday morning, proposed explanations for the empty tomb, evidence for the Resurrection, and the importance of this historical event in the life of those who choose to follow Jesus Christ.

THE FIRST EASTER SUNDAY

The uniqueness of the gospel is the resurrection of Christ. Other religions have various holy books, strong moral values, and even concepts about life after death. Every other religion contains a record of the death of their leader. But only Christianity has a God who became a man, died on a cross for all people, and was raised again in power and glory. Only Jesus Christ is alive; all the other religious leaders are dead. That fact of the Resurrection is crucial for believers living in the twenty-first century to know and understand.

There is no complete account—with all the details of the Resurrection—contained in one single Gospel. Each writer gives us a distinct look with a different emphasis that fits with their particular book. However, by putting the four Gospels together, we can see a composite picture of the Resurrection. For our present purposes, let's begin by examining the account found in the twenty-fourth chapter of Luke's Gospel:

> On the first day of the week, very early in the morning, the women took the spices they had prepared and went to the tomb. They found the stone rolled away from the tomb, but when they entered, they did not find the body of the Lord Jesus. While they were wondering about this, suddenly two men in clothes that gleamed like lightning stood beside them. In their fright the women bowed down with their faces to the ground, but the men said to them, "Why do you look for the living among the dead? He is not here; he has risen! Remember how he told you, while he was still with you in Galilee: 'The Son of Man must be delivered into the hands of sinful men, be crucified and on the third day be raised again.'" Then they remembered his words. (Luke 24:1–8)

Just imagine what it must have been like for the followers of Jesus that first Easter weekend. Feelings of defeat on Friday, disillusionment on Saturday, and then utter amazement on Sunday. The women brought spices to Jesus' tomb both as a sign of respect and to embalm his body. In those days, a body was usually embalmed at the time of burial, not a few days later. In this situation, Jesus died only a few hours before sundown on Friday, which was when the Sabbath began. By the time Joseph of Arimathea finally received the needed permission from Pilate to take Jesus' body, there was no time left to do the embalming. As required by law, the women had gone home to obey the Sabbath from sundown Friday to sundown Saturday. They gathered up their spices early Sunday morning and returned to the tomb.

When they arrived, the stone was rolled away and the tomb was empty. Keep in mind that the stone was not rolled away to let Jesus out; he was already gone. It was rolled away to let the women and the others in the tomb. It must have been a very emotional time for the women. First they discovered that the body of Jesus was missing. Then they were overwhelmed by two angels. Next came the crucial question, "Why are you looking for someone who is alive among the dead?" What a great question! Why did the women, as well as Peter and John, come running to the tomb? Because they didn't actually believe that Jesus Christ would come back from the dead! The Bible makes it clear that Jesus told his followers repeatedly that he was going to Jerusalem to die and that he would come back to life three days later.

The empty tomb is an obvious proof of the Resurrection. If Jesus didn't rise from the grave, then someone took the body. Think about this scenario for a minute. If his opponents took it, then why didn't they produce it later? It would have been impossible for the disciples to have taken Jesus' body considering the fact that a group of elite Roman soldiers had been assigned to guard the tomb, which had been locked with an official government seal that could not easily be broken.

The actions of Jesus' followers shouldn't surprise us. Look around you—at work, at school, or in your neighborhood. How many people today spend their time looking for God in dead things and in lifeless ways? They practice religion. They go to church as if it's a memorial service and read the Bible as if it's some dusty, ancient artifact. However, this is not what Christianity is all about. Because Jesus has risen from the grave, we can have a personal relationship with the living God! This is the identical God who is in the business of changing lives through the same power that raised Jesus from the dead. Have you been changed? Is the Resurrection power a reality in your life? The resurrection of Jesus from the dead is the central fact of Christianity. Without it there would be no Christian faith or church today.

But let's take it one step further. If Jesus of Nazareth actually did rise from the dead—fulfilling one of the boldest statements he ever made—then all of the other doctrinal statements he made hold together, including the ones that involve our own ultimate eternal destiny. The Resurrection gives us not only power but also confidence in the reliability of other things that Jesus said and taught.

SKEPTICS AND EVIDENCE

The evidence that Jesus actually died and rose from the grave confirms his uniqueness and proves that he is the Son of God. No one else in history has ever been able to predict his own resurrection and then fulfill it. The fact of the empty tomb was not the result of some scheme to make his resurrection plausible. Any attempt to refute it is confronted with mounds of evidence, beginning with Christ's documented appearances.

After his resurrection, Jesus appeared many times to different people. Taking all four Gospels into account, here is a chronological order of the Lord's appearances:

- Resurrection Sunday: To Mary Magdalene (John 20:14–18); the women coming back from the tomb with the angels' message (Matt. 28:8–10); in the afternoon to Peter (Luke 24:34; 1 Cor. 15:5); toward evening to the disciples on the road to Emmaus (Luke 24:13–31); all the apostles except Thomas (Luke 24:36–43; John 20:19–24).
- Eight days later: To the apostles, including Thomas (John 20:24–29).

- In Galilee: At the Lake of Tiberias to the seven (John 21:1–23); to the apostles and five hundred others on a mountain (1 Cor. 15:6).
- At Jerusalem and Bethany (a second time): To James (1 Cor. 15:7); to the eleven (Matt. 28:16–20; Mark 16:14–20; Luke 24:33–53; Acts 1:3–12).
- To Paul: Near Damascus (Acts 9:3–6; 1 Cor. 15:8); in the temple (Acts 22:17–21; 23:11).
- To Stephen outside Jerusalem (Acts 7:55).
- To John on the island of Patmos (Rev. 1:10–19).

Stop for just a moment. Let the evidence you have just read sink in. Jesus only appeared to his followers. For the most part his appearances were infrequent, with only four after Easter and before his ascension. There was nothing fantastic or far-fetched in his appearances, and they were all different in nature—in the places they occurred, the length of time involved, the words spoken, and even the mood of the apostles. All Christ's appearances were bodily in nature because Jesus wanted the disciples to be sure of this fact (Luke 24:39–40; John 20:27).

It's absolutely amazing to think that so many people, on different days and in distinct situations, all had encounters with the risen Christ. Yet despite this incredible evidence of Christ's appearances, skeptics persist in saying these records are false; they try to excuse away the Resurrection.

One such excuse is the "Vision Theory." Skeptics say there was a psychological need to create such a mental and emotional state. In this case it was a burning desire on the part of the disciples to once again see Jesus. However, such an expectation didn't have time to develop in apostolic company. Once again, look at the evidence. The women who went to the tomb early Easter morning had planned to anoint a dead body, not a risen Lord. When they saw Jesus, they were frightened and thought they had seen a spirit. Jesus immediately and conclusively shattered their misconceptions. He did the same thing with the disciples on the road to Emmaus.

These appearances were not filled with abnormal experiences or outlandish visions. The early church did not gather for ecstatic experiences. Finally, these appearances occurred rarely and stopped suddenly when Jesus was taken back up to heaven (Acts 1:22).

Another excuse that skeptics like to use in attempting to explain away the Resurrection is the "Telegraph Theory." According to this theory, Jesus telegraphed a picture of himself in bodily form back from heaven to his followers. Supposedly, these pictures were so good that they actually convinced the disciples they had seen the risen Lord. However, this theory cannot be reconciled with the actual accounts of Jesus' appearances. Take for example the encounter with the two disciples on the road to Emmaus. To believe this theory, Jesus would have had to take a picture of himself walking along a road in heaven, telegraphed the picture down to earth, and kept it steadily moving.

Then he would have needed to do the same thing with a picture of himself sitting at a long table and breaking bread. And don't forget the conversation he would have had to telegraph down to earth to convince the disciples he was actually eating with them. But all accounts clearly indicate that Jesus was truly in their midst. Either he was a master of deception or the accounts are true.

A widely circulated third view is the "Swoon Theory." Here the skeptics say that Christ never really died on the cross. Rather, he only passed out or "swooned," suffering from loss of blood, pain, and shock. Because of lack of medical knowledge, the apostles thought he was dead. When he was placed in the borrowed tomb of Joseph of Arimathea, he was still alive. Later Jesus was revived by the cool air of the tomb, and then he got up and left. His disciples insisted that it was a resurrection, not a mere resuscitation.

But this theory does not stand up either. First, consider all that Jesus had gone through in the hours leading up to the crucifixion—the terrible scourging, the exhausting journey to Calvary. Then add to this being nailed to a cross and being worn away by six hours of suffering. Consumed with exhaustion and thirst, the

Bible says he breathed his last. Just to make sure that Jesus was dead, a Roman soldier pierced his side with a spear.

More evidence that refutes this "swoon" theory includes the seal on the tomb, the Roman guard, and the stone that was rolled away. The door of the tomb could not be opened without breaking the official seal of Roman authority and power. Guards were specifically left at the tomb to protect this stamp. The guards who had kept watch were in big trouble. They were as good as finished after the stone had been rolled away. They couldn't even use the excuse that they were asleep, because sleeping on your watch meant certain death.

It takes more faith to believe these outlandish theories than it does the truth of the biblical accounts of Jesus' postresurrection appearances. What do you believe? Are you still a skeptic at heart or have you settled this debate for yourself by examining the evidence? A skeptic will never truly experience the freedom that comes from knowing Christ and the power of his resurrection until he truly believes.

MORE EVIDENCE

As we continue to refute the theories of skeptics, we build our case stronger for the resurrection of Jesus Christ. Let's examine some additional evidence. Living in a skeptical and confusing world makes it even more important for us to know the facts of this unique event in human history.

The nature of the resurrected body is an amazing mystery. On the one hand, the resurrected body of Jesus was the body of a man. On the road to Emmaus, the two disciples did not recognize Jesus (Luke 24:15–16) even though he was walking alongside them. Standing outside the tomb, Mary Magdalene did not recognize Jesus and thought he was the gardener until he called her by name (John 20:14–15). Later Jesus showed the disciples his hands, feet, and side (John 20:20, 27). On one occasion Jesus even ate a piece of broiled fish—though not out of necessity—in the presence of the disciples (Luke 24:42–43).

On the other hand, the resurrected body of Jesus had super-natural qualities. He rose with an eternal body, never to die again. After his resurrection, Jesus was able to pass through different kinds of matter: the grave linens, the tomb (without the stone being rolled away), and even the walls of the room where the disciples were meeting on Easter Sunday night. Jesus was also able to instantly vanish from their midst (Luke 24:31). And in this same body, Jesus ascended into heaven. Although we are not given all the details as to exactly how Jesus' body was changed after his resurrection, it was still clearly identifiable as the one put in the tomb. Jesus' resurrection body served as a prototype for believers as well. Our resurrection bodies will be different from our earthly ones, just as Jesus was. They will be new, yet related to our former bodies (1 Cor. 15:35–41).

There is another proof for the Resurrection that is rarely mentioned, yet it offers some interesting evidence to consider. Look at this account from John 20:3–8.

So Peter and the other disciple [John] started for the tomb. Both were running, but the other disciple outran Peter and reached the tomb first. He bent over and looked in at the strips of linen lying there but did not go in. Then Simon Peter, who was behind him, arrived and went into the tomb. He saw the strips of linen lying there, as well as the burial cloth that had been around Jesus' head. The cloth was folded up by itself, separate from the linen. Finally the other disciple, who had reached the tomb first, also went inside. He saw and believed.

The disciples saw how the linen wrappings still retained the shape of a body and how the headpiece was in another place by itself. No one could have taken the body out of the wrappings and have them maintain the shape of a body. There could only be one explanation: The body of Jesus had passed through the wrappings! If you have ever wondered if the Shroud of Turin was the actual burial cloth of Jesus, the above passage from John 20 should answer that question for you.

All the Gospels also record the presence of angels at one particular time following Jesus' resurrection early Sunday morning (Matt. 28:1–8; Mark 16:5–8; Luke 24:3–9, 22–23; John 20:11–13). This closely follows other accounts of the presence of angels with Christ, including the birth of Christ and his temptation in the wilderness. This was another way God made it clear Jesus was his Son and had been raised from the grave.

When considering evidence for the Resurrection, we must also look at the transformed apostles. A profound and permanent change came over the apostles during the days following Easter morning. The only possible way to explain this phenomenal change is that the apostles were thoroughly convinced that Jesus had risen from the grave. The cowardice they experienced just before the Crucifixion was gone, replaced with a new courage that would endure many years until their martyrdom. Look at the difference in Peter from John 19 to Acts 2. Knowledge of the Resurrection made that difference!

They went everywhere and preached Christ and his resurrection. Their reward was persecution, torment, incarceration, and execution. Nothing could have driven them and their successors to the ends of the earth through these kinds of ordeals but the conviction that Christ had indeed been raised from the dead by the Father and was therefore the Son of God. The Holy Spirit honored their convictions about the Resurrection and communicated the gospel through them with great power (Acts 4:33). As a result, their faith became contagious, and Jews and Gentiles alike were convinced that Jesus had risen. The preaching of the Resurrection turned the world upside down. The early apostles took the fact that they had been commissioned to be "witnesses" very seriously (Luke 24:48; Acts 1:8).

Another interesting consequence of the Resurrection was the change in the observance of the Lord's Day. This shift in the day of worship was recorded in the New Testament and has continued through the centuries. The move from Saturday—the seventh day, religiously observed by Jews throughout the world from early times—to Sunday was a big one. Suddenly and uniformly Christians began to worship on Sunday, even though it was an ordinary workday (Acts 20:7). They did this because they wanted to commemorate the resurrection of their Lord, which took place on a Sunday. The phrase "the first day of the week" is not found in the Bible until the dawn of Easter. It is introduced by New Testament writers and is carried through in the following passages: Matthew 28:1; Mark 16:2; Luke 24:1; John 20:1; Acts 20:7; and 1 Corinthians 16:2.

With this kind of overwhelming evidence to support the resurrection of Jesus Christ, it's hard to conceive that anyone could still be a skeptic. After reading this chapter I hope you will recognize, in a new way, the importance of the Resurrection to the Christian faith and to your own walk with Jesus.

THE IMPORTANCE OF THE RESURRECTION

The Gospels do not explain the Resurrection; the Resurrection explains the Gospels. Belief in the Resurrection is not an appendage to the Christian faith; it is the Christian faith. —John S. Whale[1]

The most important part of the gospel is the resurrection of Christ. Without this, everything else becomes meaningless, including the death of Christ. Romans 4:25 reminds us that Jesus was "delivered over to death for our sins and was raised to life for our justification." In his death he took on our sins, but in his resurrection he guaranteed us entrance into heaven.

To fully grasp the importance of the Resurrection, it would be good for us to clearly define it. The Resurrection mentioned in the Scriptures is physical, not spiritual. In the original language of the New Testament Greek, the word used for *resurrection* is *anastasis nekron*. This literally means the "standing up of a corpse." Thus *resurrection* in the Bible means "to stand up," and it always refers to the body. Author and Oxford scholar C. S. Lewis used to debate with the liberals of his day in England regarding their position that the Resurrection was only spiritual. Lewis would ask, "What position does a spirit take when it stands up?"

Just think about the promise that is ours. One day our dead bodies are going to "stand up" from the grave! When Paul writes about the Resurrection in 1 Corinthians 15, he is not talking about a spiritual resurrection because the soul never dies. The moment a body dies, the soul goes somewhere. According to 2 Corinthians 5:6–8, the minute a child of God is absent from the body, he is in the presence of the Lord. The fantastic thing about the Christian faith is that we never view death as the end. Instead, we look into eternity and see the hope that is offered through the resurrected life of Jesus Christ.

Let's look more closely at 1 Corinthians 15:1–8, where Paul writes about the proof of the Resurrection and its prominence in the gospel.

> Now, brothers, I want to remind you of the gospel I preached to you, which you received and on which you have taken your stand. By this gospel you are saved, if you hold firmly to the word I preached to you. Otherwise, you have believed in vain.
>
> For what I received I passed on to you as of first importance: that Christ died for our sins according to the Scriptures, that he was buried, that he was raised on the third day according to the Scriptures, and that he appeared to Peter, and then to the Twelve. After that, he appeared to more than five hundred of the brothers at the same time, most of whom are still living, though some have fallen asleep. Then he appeared to James, then to all the apostles, and last of all he appeared to me also, as to one abnormally born.

Paul declares that he is a communicator of the gospel. The gospel—"good news"—contains three essential facts: Jesus died for you and me, he was buried, and he rose again. There is no gospel apart from these facts. Notice there is nothing that we must do. Rather it tells us what Jesus has already done for us. It's great news that Christ died and rose again, that he just didn't vanish. His tomb is empty and he is alive today. This gospel is not only great news, but it also has the power to change lives. Has your life been transformed by the "good news"? Are you sharing this life-changing message with others?

A few verses later in 1 Corinthians 15, Paul puts down a series of "ifs" as a demonstration of the importance of the resurrection of Jesus Christ. There was no question in Paul's mind that Christ might not have risen from the dead. Let's examine these "ifs" in light of the importance of the Resurrection.

1. "If there is no resurrection of the dead, then not even Christ has been raised" (v. 13). The resurrection of the dead and Christ's rising are linked together. Later in this chapter we read that based on his resurrection, Christ is the firstfruits and there will be more to follow—for those who have placed their faith in him.

2. "And if Christ has not been raised, our preaching is useless and so is your faith" (v. 14). Not only is our preaching in vain, but so is our faith if Christ has not risen from the dead physically. You might as well stop going to church and reading your Bible. There is no reason to do any of this if Christ was not raised from the grave.

3. "More than that, we are then found to be false witnesses about God, for we have testified about God that he raised Christ from the dead. But he did not raise him if in fact the dead are not raised" (v. 15). Men do not die for what they know to be a lie. There are some men who have died for a lie when they thought it was the truth. For instance, think of the millions who died for Communism because they believed in their leaders. The apostles declared that they had seen the risen Christ and were willing to die for that proclamation.

4. "For if the dead are not raised, then Christ has not been raised either. And if Christ has not been raised, your faith is futile; you are still in your sins. Then those also who have fallen asleep in Christ are lost" (vv. 16–18). If Christ has not conquered death, then we are all in big trouble. This means that we are all destined for a Christless eternity in hell. There is no hope of eternal life. Think of the multiplied millions of believers who have died trusting Christ as their Savior. If Jesus has not risen, than every single one of them has perished.

5. "If only for this life we have hope in Christ, we are to be pitied more than all men" (v. 19). Christianity is not just a religion for this life, it is a relationship for eternity. If in fact Christ had not conquered death, then we have been deceived and are the most miserable people on the planet. But we are not distressed; instead, we celebrate because Jesus is alive!

The resurrection of Christ means that God gave his approval to the claims and works of Jesus. These claims would have been blasphemous if Jesus were not truly the Son of God. However, the Resurrection authenticates Jesus and his teaching. The empty tomb should assure us forever that all the things that Jesus taught were true. If Christ had not risen from the dead, then he would not be alive to do all his postresurrection work. We would not have a High Priest, Advocate, Head of the church, or Intercessor. Ultimately, there would be no living Person to indwell and empower us (Rom. 6:1–10; Gal. 2:20).

As Christians, however, we know the truth. In the resurrected Christ we have power for living today and hope for all our tomorrows.

CHAPTER 6

Whatever Happened to Easter Vacation?

Easter is beginning to look a lot like Christmas. The Easter bunny appears to be taking on the persona of Santa Claus, leading the call to commercialization and "charge it!" There are some who continue to say that Easter is the last bastion when it comes to religious holidays, but don't buy into that reasoning too quickly. In recent years, Easter appears to have taken on many of the same trappings as Christmas.

Take for example the yard decorations. Plastic bunnies, Easter trees, and even trees decorated with brightly colored eggs are all becoming more prevalent. The marketing specialists at Hallmark Card Corporation carefully studied the way Americans celebrate holidays so as to detect new trends that are developing. In response to the public's growing desire for a fuller Easter holiday experience, Hallmark has brought out hundreds of new decorating items and gifts. These include plastic eggs, bunnies, ducks, and other items to be attached to Easter wreaths and to be hung on Easter trees. There are even windsocks, adorned with a variety of designs, to dance in the wind.

Parents are wanting to give their children a meaningful Easter. This has resulted in a number of growing traditions like the Easter wreath. People either buy straw wreaths from a local florist or fashion one themselves out of grapevines or twigs woven together. The wreaths can be hung on a front door, placed on a mantle, or set flat

71

in the center of a table. These table centerpieces are often ringed with small candles or with a large candle stuck right in the middle.

Gifts designed to give at Easter time come in a variety of shapes and sizes, for all age groups. There is everything from T-shirts and hats to smaller items that are similar to those used to stuff in Christmas socks. The traditional Easter basket has evolved into an elaborate gift item containing assorted jelly beans, chocolate bunnies, and stuffed animals. There are even Easter baskets available for your pets.

Another tradition growing in popularity seems to have a direct correlation to a Santa Claus custom: dressing up as the Easter bunny for a picture at the mall or to entertain children at a party. Each year costume shops see an increasing demand for furry rabbit outfits. Even hotels now use costumed bunnies to entertain guests.

While it is true that Easter has yet to reach the same level of commercialization as that of Christmas, it has still been greatly influenced by our culture, to the point where it is no longer a strictly religious holiday. Just pick up a local newspaper the week before Easter and see how little space is devoted to the death and resurrection of Jesus Christ (other than the religious page, if there is one). Instead, you will find column after column advertising deals on Easter feasts from local restaurants. And whether you want an Easter champagne brunch or sugar-free Easter candy for dessert, it's all available for you to enjoy. Now don't get me wrong; I'm not being an Easter Scrooge. There's nothing wrong with enjoying a delicious meal with family and friends in a nice restaurant, as long as we remember why and what we are celebrating.

But the reality is, we are looking at a culture that is gradually moving away from Judeo-Christian values to one that is pluralistic. We seem to be on a course designed to remove God from every dimension of societal life, from commerce to education.

NO MORE HAPPY EASTER

Take, for example, shopping at a grocery market, mall, or department store at Easter time. The stores are jammed with shoppers buying decorations and candy. Cash registers are ringing, and customers are streaming through the doors loaded down with packages. But in most malls and stores you can search in vain for an important word—*Jesus,* and sometimes even *Easter.* They are basically nowhere to be found.

There are no banners proclaiming "He's Alive" or "He Has Risen." There's hardly a cross to be found. Few stores, if any, wish their customers a "Happy Easter" with a banner or a word. Easter decorations are plentiful, but somehow most department store and mall decorators omit any explicitly Christian allusions. Big department stores seem to carefully avoid Easter rhetoric in their holiday season slogans. In a way they are helping the world forget why we even have a spring Easter holiday.

Obviously this is all quite deliberate. It is an attempt by commercial America to obliterate the memory, custom by custom, image by image, word by word, of Easter. Why? Probably the biggest reason has to do with the age of tolerance in which we are living; no one wants to "offend" anybody. Have you noticed that the message of tolerance seems to apply to every lifestyle and philosophy *except* Christianity?

Yet, it goes even deeper than that. More and more, it appears that the very existence of Christianity seems to pose increasing problems for those attempting to manage our society. This is becoming apparent in many dimensions, including our educational system.

NO MORE EASTER VACATION

In the last few years there has been a conscious effort to remove God from our public schools, even when it comes to Easter. One example of this is changing "Easter vacation" to "Spring break." Traditional customs and stories mentioning Christ are said to violate students' rights and are no longer permitted. However, the impact goes well beyond just the Easter holiday.

My twins, Tony and Kati, were required to listen to a presentation by two Muslims in their seventh-grade social studies class. No other world religions were presented on such a personal level.

Thirty percent of their required textbook reading for the class had to do with the history of Islam. Part of the in-class work that Tony and Kati did was to make an Islamic prayer book. Tony was also a member of the school Pentathlon Team, which competed against other middle schools in our area of southern California. Part of his required preparation for the debate questions included studying Hinduism and evolution. There wasn't any mention or any material that had to do with Christianity whatsoever.

Yet, when I was invited to present a "Real Answers" assembly at their middle school, I found it rather ironic (on Good Friday no less) that the principal made it extremely clear prior to my presentation that under no condition could I mention God, Jesus, or the Bible. She concluded her "briefing" by making sure that I fully understood the laws governing the separation of church and state. At that point I didn't feel it was necessary to inform her that these laws had been misinterpreted. I have run into this same thing countless times across the United States and Canada as I speak on public school campuses each year. Whatever happened to equal access or "non-bias" tolerance? More importantly, why are people so afraid of the Jesus of Easter?

New Age philosophies and eastern mysticism are being brought into our classrooms while God is being shown the exit door. Even Halloween is celebrated in some form on most school campuses. Public education has changed dramatically in the last two and a half decades. Gone are the days of the traditional three Rs—reading, 'riting and 'rithmetic. A fourth R has now been added: reproductive rights. And it's impacting even elementary schools. A *Washington Times* article included the story of a seven-year-old boy who had to be comforted by his teacher because he thought a girl in his class had insulted him. She called him a virgin. The teacher asked whether he knew what the word meant. "No," replied the little boy, "but I know it's something horrible." Is it any wonder our kids are more confused than ever today?

Schools have become battlefields for a wide array of causes and issues: school-based clinics, values clarification, evolution, self-esteem, and gay awareness. A homosexual teachers' group in

Massachusetts exposed teenagers as young as fourteen to graphic "how-to" descriptions of sex acts that were so indecent they could not even be mentioned in the local newspaper. Then there was the human rights campaign that sponsored a West Coast conference featuring porn star Annie Sprinkle, the showing of hard-core porn films to students, and a prostitute's workshop. Our schools' drop-out rate continues to increase in some regions of the country, and we are just beginning to wake up to the literacy problem.

New stress has been added as teachers and administrators feel the pressure to improve test scores by fixing the numbers. In suburban Potomac, Maryland, an elementary school principal resigned after parents complained their children were coached to give right answers on state tests. Ohio state officials investigated charges of cheating by teachers at a Columbus elementary school. This was the same school that had previously received praise from President Clinton for raising test scores. In New York City, more than twenty-four administrators and teachers from thirty different schools were accused of urging students to cheat on a variety of standard city and state tests.

In some places school officials can lose their jobs if their students don't produce the right numbers on standardized tests. In other parts of the country, educators can get as much as a $25,000 bonus if they can raise students' test scores. These tests can determine everything from whether a child gets promoted to the annual budget of a school district. It's bad enough when students get kicked out for cheating, but now an alarming number of administrators and teachers are facing charges for fixing numbers.[2]

Abraham Lincoln said, "The philosophy of education in one generation will be the philosophy of government in the next." Public education influences the greatest number of people in the most thorough way at the most impressionable age. Just what philosophy are our children being taught in the classroom today? What values are they assimilating—and from where—to help them deal with the stages of life? We have a generation at risk.

We could continue to look at what is happening in education, for there is much we would be able to examine. However, I have covered this issue rather extensively in three previous books (see "Ministry Information" on p. 153). I encourage you to read them if you would like further information on the shift in education in our society.

Instead, let's look at the changes in our culture from two additional angles, the first one being more of a historical perspective on the change in the fabric of our society and the second on how the lifestyle of Christians has impacted our world, in a negative way.

DOES GOD HAVE REAL ANSWERS FOR OUR SOCIETY?

In many of our citywide evangelistic crusades, we conduct special "interest group" meetings. These evangelistic meetings target groups of people who have an affinity to one another, whether through gender, profession, or some other common denominator. While conducting a crusade in Norman, Oklahoma, we had a special outreach to a group of people that we had never targeted before in this way: professors. A special luncheon was put together where I was then asked to address the question, "Does God have any real answers for our society?" We had a marvelous time, with much positive response from those who attended. In doing the research for my message, I was reminded in a fresh way just how far our society has traveled from its Judeo-Christian roots.

I began my talk with a story about a relative of mine who was a judge in northern California. Judge William Porter Gutherie was known for some rather unorthodox practices on the bench. For example, he never sentenced a juvenile offender to jail. Their sentence was to attend the church of their choice on Sunday, write a report, and turn it into him on Tuesday. Judge Gutherie felt more could be accomplished in Sunday school and church than in jail. At the time of his death, my family received letters from people all over the country thanking the judge for his sentence and what it had done in their lives. Some who wrote held high-level jobs with the government and would never have been able to secure their positions with a criminal record.

This type of sentencing would be unheard of today. What has caused the fabric of our society to change so dramatically? Today political and social leaders struggle with seemingly insurmountable problems like violent crime, a climbing divorce rate, teen pregnancy, illegal drug use, AIDS, and illiteracy. Maybe it's because of the changing role Christianity has had in our society since the inception of our nation. It could be that we are paying the price for exiling religion from public life.

How did our founding fathers feel about religion—more specifically Christianity—and public life? Oftentimes today we hear that our founding fathers were atheists, agnostics, and deists. But this is not accurate. The majority of our founding fathers (fifty-two out of fifty-five) were Christians. Take for example the following men and their position on Christianity:

- Benjamin Franklin: "Whoever will introduce into public affairs the principles of Christianity, will change the face of the world."
- Patrick Henry (credited with the famous statement "Give me liberty or give me death"): "It cannot be emphasized too strongly or too often, that this great nation was founded not by religionists, but by Christians; not on religions, but on the gospel of Jesus Christ."

Statements like these used to be common in school history textbooks. Patrick Henry's was found in one published by the American Tract Society in 1813. Today this group is known for publishing religious literature, but in the formative years of our nation it was one of the leading publishers of school textbooks.

There were other books, like the *New England Primer* (1795 version), that used to teach students their ABCs and reading. About a quarter of the way through the book, a phrase was put with each letter. Students memorized the phrases, which happened to be Bible verses. Here are a couple of samples:

C–"Come unto me, all ye that labour and are heavy laden, and I will give you rest" (Matt. 11:28 KJV).

E–"Except a man be born again, he cannot see the kingdom of God" (John 3:3 KJV).

This book was first introduced in America in 1690, and it was used until 1900. Today it would be the equivalent of a first-grade reader. It's interesting to see how much our attitudes have changed in education over the years.

And what about the system of government our founding fathers gave to us? It's one that has been remarkably successful for more than two hundred years under the same document, the Constitution. No other modern nation can make this claim. In the last two hundred years, France has had seven completely different forms of government, while Italy has had some fifty. But we are still in our first. How did our government get put together in such a unique and lasting way?

Political science professors at the University of Houston wanted to know where our founding fathers got their ideas. They decided that if they collected some of their writings and knew who they quoted, they would then know where their ideas came from. So they collected more than 15,000 of the founding fathers' writings, then narrowed them down to 3,154 writings that they felt had a significant impact on the thinking of the founding fathers of America.

It took ten years to thoroughly examine these writings. The professors concluded that the three most often quoted people were Blackstone, Montesquieu, and John Locke. Moreover, they discovered something else they had not expected. Of the *sources* that were quoted, four times more often than Montesquieu, twelve times more often than Blackstone, and sixteen times more often than Locke the founding fathers quoted the Bible. Thirty-four percent of the quotes came directly out of the Bible, and another 60 percent were from other men who had used the Bible to arrive at their conclusions.

Another interesting thing they found was that the idea for the three branches of our government came from Isaiah 33:22. The constitutionally protected separation of powers, to keep each branch independent, came from Jeremiah 17. Our founding fathers were firmly convinced of the value of integrating biblical principles in government.

So who were some of these men? Blackstone wrote *Commentaries on the Laws of England* (first introduced to America in 1758). For more than 160 years it was the most important law textbook used in America. Essentially it was the Bible for lawyers. The Supreme Court quoted from it regularly. Where did Blackstone get his ideas? Every time he gave the laws, he gave the Bible verses on which the laws were based. Charles Finney, one of the great evangelists of the early 1800s—like an early Billy Graham—hadn't planned to be in the ministry. Rather, he had studied to be a lawyer. In the process of studying Blackstone's commentaries, however, he became a Christian and decided to go into the ministry.

John Quincy Adams spent eighteen years in the House of Representatives. At the age of fourteen, he received a diplomatic appointment to the court of Catherine the Great in Russia. Yet he was a very committed believer in Christ. He once said, "The highest glory of the American Revolution was this, it connected in one dissoluble bond the principles of civil government with the principles of Christianity."

John Jay was the first chief justice of the Supreme Court. He was also one of the three men most responsible for our Constitution. According to Jay, "Providence has given to our people the choice of their rulers, and it is the duty as well as the privilege and interest of our Christian nation to select and prefer Christians for their rulers."

How long has it been since we have heard anything close to this sentiment from our Supreme Court?

So when did all the change begin? We need to go back to the year 1801. The Danbury Baptist Association of Danbury, Connecticut, heard a rumor that the Congregational denomination was about to be made the official denomination of America. This distressed the Baptists, so they fired off a letter to President Thomas Jefferson and expressed their concerns.

On January 1, 1802, Jefferson wrote to them and assured them that the First Amendment had erected a wall between church and state. But the wall was one-directional—it was designed to keep government from running the church, yet it assured that Christian principles would always remain in government. He made it clear that God's principles were to stay in government, but government was to stay out of the church.

Things remained this way for many years in spite of challenges along the way. In 1844, a school in Philadelphia said, "We are going to teach our kids morality, but we don't need the Bible or religion to do it." This was such an unorthodox position for that day that the case made it to the Supreme Court. The ruling for the case *Vidal* vs. *Girard* included the following: "Why may not the Bible and especially the New Testament be read and taught as a divine revelation in the schools? Where can the purest principles of morality be learned so clearly or so perfectly as from the New Testament?" You can't teach morality without Christianity.

In 1853, a small group petitioned Congress and said they wanted a complete separation of Christian principles from government. The petition was referred to the House and Senate Judiciary Committee, and it was investigated for one year to see if it was possible to separate Christianity from government. Here's their ruling: "Had the people during the Revolution had any suspicion of any attempt to war against Christianity, that revolution would have been strangled in its cradle. At the time of the adoption of the Constitution and the amendments, the universal sentiment was that Christianity should be encouraged, not any one sect. In this age there can be no substitute for Christianity. That was the religion of the founding fathers of the republic and they expected it to remain the religion of their descendants."

Still more challenges came in the 1870s, 1880s, and 1890s. In 1878 the Supreme Court heard the case of *Reynolds* vs. *United States*. The Court went back and pulled out Jefferson's letter in its entirety and quoted it: "Yes, Jefferson said there was to be a separation of church and state, but it was to protect the church from the government. Jefferson also said that Christian principles were also never to be separated from government."

Another similar case came to the Supreme Court in 1892 in *Church of the Holy Trinity* vs. *United States*. Their conclusion: "Our laws and our institutions must necessarily be based upon and embody the teaching of the Redeemer of mankind. It is impossible for it to be otherwise, and in this sense and to this extent, our civilization and our institutions are emphatically Christian." They gave a sixteen-page ruling citing eighty-seven precedents based on the founding fathers and other cases.

The Court made it clear that the First Amendment was never intended to separate Christian principles from government, yet today we often hear about the separation of church and state. In fact, in one poll 67 percent of Americans surveyed said they thought it was actually a part of the First Amendment. The First Amendment actually states: "Congress shall make no law respecting an establishment of religion, or prohibiting the free exercise thereof."

In 1947, for the first time in the Court's history, only eight words were used out of Jefferson's speech. In the case of *Everson* vs. *Board of Education,* the Court quoted the following: "The first amendment has erected a wall between church and state. That wall must be kept high and impregnable." This was first time a case like this had ever been reversed in America. All previous interpretations stated that the wall was designed to protect church from government, but now it was used to protect government from church. It was a new philosophy for the Court. Why and where did it come from?

The members of the Court were influenced by a man named Dr. William James, who is often called the "father of modern psychology." He was a strong opponent of religious principles in both education and government. His position can be summed up in the following statement: "There is nothing so absurd, but if you repeat it often enough, people will believe it."

In a historic case, *Engle* vs. *Vitale* (June 25, 1962), a short prayer was removed from schools by the Court. The twenty-two word prayer in question was "Almighty God, we acknowledge our dependence upon thee and we beg thy blessings upon us, our parents, our teachers, and our country." There were no precedents, nor any historical or legal basis for this decision. Within twelve months (by June 17, 1963), the Court had completely removed prayer, Bible reading, and religious instruction from the classroom. In the case of *Abington* vs. *Schempp,* the reason the Court gave for removing prayer and religious instruction was: "If portions of the New Testament were read without explanation, they could be and had been psychologically harmful to the mind" (once again, there was no historical or legal base for this statement).

Eight years later, when the court was talking about the prayer, they said it was a "To Whom It May Concern" prayer. At that time polls showed 97 percent of the American people believed in God and only 3 percent said they did not. Yet the Court sided with the 3 percent. This was the first time in American history that 3 percent became a majority.

What affect has all this had on our society since the 1963 ruling? Let's look at the four general areas mentioned in the supposedly "unconstitutional prayer."

1. Students. George Washington once said, "Reason and experience both forbid us to expect that national morality can prevail in exclusion of religious principles."

The case of *Stone* vs. *Graham,* in 1980, challenged the right of students to see the Ten Commandments while in school. The Court's ruling: "If the posted copies of the Ten Commandments are to have any effect at all, it will be to induce the school children to read, meditate upon, perhaps to venerate and obey the Commandments. This is not a permissible objective."

Concepts like honor thy father and mother, thou shall not kill, and thou shall not steal were now not desirable for young people to think about. Just look at the consequences in our society. Imagine if the Ten Commandments had come from anywhere else—Aristotle, Plato, Socrates—then they would have been allowed without question. Keep in mind that when the Court says something is unconstitutional, they are saying that our founding fathers would not have wanted nor intended for this to happen. Yet consider the thoughts of James Madison, the one man most responsible for the content of the Constitution: "We have staked the whole future of American civilization not on the power of government, far from it. We have staked the future of all our political institutions upon the capacity of each and all of us to govern ourselves according to the Ten Commandments of God."

While the Court was busy guarding young people from too much religious influence, look at some statistics corresponding to the same time period. Teen pregnancy among fifteen- to nineteen-year-old girls was almost level from 1951–1963. Then it dramatically increased: there was a 533 percent increase in pregnancy and STDs among ten- to fourteen-year-old girls, and in fifteen- to nineteen-year-olds there was a 226 percent increase.

2. Families and Parents. For fifteen consecutive years, divorce had been declining in America. After 1963, it shot up 117 percent. I saw this in my own extended family. While attending a family reunion, my mother's generation of cousins was asked to fill in a chart of their children, spouses, and so forth. (This was a continuation of a family tree going back to my great-great-great grandparents.) There was not enough room on the chart because of all the divorces and remarriages. Ironically, my mother's generation was the first to turn from the Christian faith, which had been a strong heritage in our family for generations.

There has also been a dramatic increase in single-parent families and even unmarried couples living together.

3. Schools, Teachers, and Education. SAT tests have been around since 1926. Prior to 1963, there had never been two years in a row where scores went up or down. Scores are now so low that the Department of Education says it's the first time in U.S. history that we are graduating a generation of students who know less academically than their parents. Millions of high school graduates each year lack the ability to read at a second-grade level. Thousands of kids graduate each year from high school unable to read their diplomas.

4. Our Nation. The moral fabric of our nation is falling apart. Take violent crime for instance. There has been an increase of 544 percent since 1963. Thomas Jefferson said: "The reason Christianity is the best friend for government is because Christianity deals with the heart." The founding fathers knew that Christianity could stop crime before it happened because it focuses on the attitude of the heart. In the New Testament Jesus didn't say don't kill; he said don't hate. He didn't say don't commit adultery; rather, he said don't lust. It's pretty clear, if you don't deal with the heart, you'll deal with crime. John Adams said, "We have no government armed with power which is capable of contending with human passions unbridled by morality and religion. No government in the world is big enough to make you do what is right! Our Constitution was made only for a moral and religious people. It is wholly inadequate to the government of any other."

Maybe it's time to revisit the principles of Christianity. It's the Bible or the jungle. But this change cannot happen all at once or in huge, mass groups of people. Because we are dealing with an issue of the heart, it must start individually. The bottom line is that we must start living what we speak, and that appears to be a major hurdle to overcome in our current Christian culture. In part we, as Christians, must accept responsibility for the condition of our society. The body of Christ has been asleep for too long, and it's time to reclaim lost ground. Foundational to impacting our world is to live a distinctively different life.

LIVE WHAT YOU SPEAK

We live in a culture of creature comforts and convenience. Unfortunately, many Christians today choose to live by what is convenient rather than by the standards of God's Word. In fact, for the most part, there is basically no difference between the lifestyle of Christians and non-Christians.

Researcher George Barna has his finger on the pulse of this problem of the lifestyle of Christians. His organization did a survey among more than six thousand adults comparing the lives of self-described born-again Christians to non-Christians. The two groups were measured on sixty-six core religious practices and beliefs. The results showed that the self-described Christians were demonstrably different on only nine of those sixty-six factors. Even more revealing was that in the comparison of the two groups on sixty-five nonreligious factors, including core values, common moral behaviors, and attitudes regarding truth and ethics, the Christians were indistinguishable from the non-Christians on all sixty-five items.[3]

Maybe some of the problems in our society can be attributed to the lifestyle of Christians. Perhaps it's time to stop telling the world all the things Christians are against and start communicating what we are for. We cannot continue to acknowledge Jesus with our mouths and deny him with our lives. The single greatest barrier to evangelism today is the lifestyle of self-described Christians. So how do we fix the problem?

There is no "quick fix" or "magical formula" to remedy this problem. Our ability to live differently in a world that is confused is based, in part, on developing and maintaining right priorities: Bible study, prayer, and worship. However, there are also several other key factors involved in living differently from our culture.

Do you know your true identity, who you are in Christ? Are you living it? If we are truly followers of Jesus Christ, our lives should be markedly different. The apostle Paul gives us some vivid word pictures of this contrast in 2 Corinthians 5:17: "Therefore, if anyone is in Christ, he is a new creation; the old has gone and the new has come!" As Christians, we are brand-new people on the inside. The Holy Spirit gives us new life, and we are not the same anymore. We are not reformed, rehabilitated, or reeducated; we are new creations living in a vital relationship with Christ. After we are spiritually reborn, our old value systems, priorities, beliefs, and plans are gone. Evil and sin are still present, but they no longer dominate us.

Are you living in light of who you are, as a child of the King? Here's a simple exercise that you can do, as a reminder, to reinforce your identity in Christ. Take a three-by-five-inch card and write the following words on it: "I am a child of the King." Then place that card in a spot where you will see it several times a day. This simple tool can be a simple reminder to take account of your activities thus far in the day and see if you're living like a child of the King.

A second key component in living what you speak is developing a disciplined mind. As George Barna concluded, "Most Christians don't live differently than non-Christians because Christians don't think differently."[4] In Colossians 3:2 we read, "Set your minds on things above, not on earthly things." Because our real home is in heaven, where Christ lives, we should have a different perspective in our lives here on earth. To let heaven fill your thoughts means to look at life from God's point of view. This is the antidote to the issues of life in the twenty-first century. A rightly set mind will affect everything from how we treat family members to how we conduct our business affairs. The more we see life around us as God sees it, the more we will live a distinctively different life.

Next we must make a conscious choice to stay on God's pathway for life. King David writes about the benefits of walking along this pathway in Psalm 16:11. "You have made known to me the path of life; you will fill me with joy in your presence, with eternal pleasures at your right hand." This is the path that leads to fulfillment and meaning in life. The "What Would Jesus Do?" (WWJD) adage has become quite popular in our Christian culture today. At the heart of this saying is the principle of asking ourselves throughout the day, "What would Jesus want me to do in this situation?" We must consciously choose to be obedient to God, to stay on his pathway, and to avoid the detours of going our own—and the world's—way.

Ultimately, if we want to live differently in a crazy world, we must keep Jesus in first place in our lives, in everything we do. The same power that brought Jesus back to life on that first Easter Sunday morning is available to us to help us live a different quality of life now. The Resurrection gives us a hope for the future. Colossians 3:4 reminds us, "When Christ, who is your life, appears, then you also will appear with him in glory." In Christ, we have everything we need in life. So don't just "talk the walk," enjoy the benefits of "walking the talk" with Jesus. Nothing can compare to the difference he can make in your life.

It's time to stop talking about all the problems in our world and trying to pin the blame on someone. Let's stop living by what is convenient and start living by what is right, according to God's standards. We do not have to stand around and become victims of our society. On the flip side, we also don't have to hide in our holy huddles hoping that somehow everything will eventually come out all right. By living distinctively different, we can impact our world for the kingdom of God. Together let's change what we can and reclaim territory that has been lost to the enemy of our souls.

We have been commissioned to take this powerful message in history to a confused world. It is the message of Easter. So just don't stand there; instead, do the right thing. Let's tell the world by our words and our actions that Jesus truly is alive.

CHAPTER 7

Confronting the Cross

On Good Friday, two days before Easter, hundreds of people throughout the Philippines participate in something called the Rite of the Flagellates, a ritual that dates back many generations. While this self-inflicted punishment goes back to early human history, it was not until the early thirteenth century that flagellation as a penance became a recognized practice.

What is it? It is a reenactment of the suffering Jesus experienced leading up to and including the Crucifixion. Amazingly, some people have participated in this ritual for as many as twenty years! They don't just dramatize the events that Jesus went through; they actually relive them.

Participants begin by stripping their upper bodies of all clothing. Then they pull their arms to their chests, causing the skin on their backs to stretch tight across the muscles. Another person then strikes their bare backs with a piece of wood that resembles a large spatula. Because the device contains bits of glass, razor blades, and other sharp objects, this flogging rips open the skin, creating massive wounds similar to those Jesus would have received. The participants then continue this self-mutilation by beating themselves with a bamboo whip as they walk through the center of their town or village.

Eventually, most pass out and fall down in the dusty street. At that time a bystander comes along with a warm bottle of Coke or 7UP (water if they're really lucky) and pours it on their open wounds. This is done to revive the participants. Then the intentional victims put on brightly colored robes and carry the crossbeams on which they will be crucified, each weighing between seventy and one hundred pounds. They head through the center of town to the appointed spot where they will be crucified. At this point, they are literally nailed to the wood. Those participating in this rite then hang on a cross for anywhere from fifteen minutes to three hours.

Why would anyone want to do this to themselves? What does it accomplish?

As sincere and devoted as these people may be, they are also sincerely misinformed about how to win God's favor and what grace is all about. They do not fully understand God's love, his grace, his mercy, nor the hope of Easter. They think they need to punish themselves for their sin. Surprisingly, most who survive this entire ritual will come back the following year, and the year after that, and the year after that, and so on. If they don't continue what they have started, they're considered a disgrace to their families.

Christians who witness this event refer to it as a horrible spectacle. They want to scream out to the participants and spectators, "Stop! What you're doing is worthless in the sight of God. There is no way you can earn God's grace or satisfy him. The price has been paid already. You don't have to hang on a cross. Just receive God's love and forgiveness."

WHAT CROSS DO YOU CARRY?

Most of us wouldn't even consider beating ourselves physically or try hanging on a cross to achieve some deeper spirituality. However, sometimes we try other things to earn God's favor:

- Doing good deeds because we think it will make us more spiritual.
- Acting the "religiously correct" way around those who expect good behavior from us.
- Attending church, Christian concerts, and other related meetings.
- Putting money in the offering plate to ease an apathetic conscience.

Doing the right thing should come naturally out of our love for God and a desire to please him. However, when we do "spiritual things" to ease our conscience or to impress God, we ignore what Christ has already done on our behalf. God demonstrated the extent of his love for us through Christ's death on the cross. "But God demonstrates his own love for us in this: While we were still sinners, Christ died for us" (Rom. 5:8). Jesus came into the world for the primary reason of dying on the cross.

During the time Jesus was on the cross, God the Father placed on him all the sin of the human race for all generations. Jesus took upon himself the weight, guilt, and penalty for our sin. Jesus died, was buried, and rose on the third day, having offered his own blood to the Father as a final payment for all our sins. The Resurrection is proof that God accepted the sacrificial payment Jesus made on our behalf.

In order to better understand the importance of Christ's death on the cross, we need to start by looking at the trial that set everything in motion for the Crucifixion. Since each Gospel writer presents a slightly different view of the trial and death of Christ, we will begin by looking through the eyes of Mark. However, we will also include details from Matthew, Luke, and John.

THE TRIAL OF JESUS

At the end of Mark 14, we find Jesus in a difficult situation. He is in the hands of his enemies, and his disciples are scattered. One follower has betrayed him and another has denied him. J. Vernon McGee says that sin is the issue this night in two different ways. First, sin is trying to destroy Jesus. Secondly, he is doing something about sin: He is dying for your sin and my sin. This is the heart of the gospel. It is what Jesus did, not something God is asking us to do.

Jesus has been forced to endure a multistaged illegal trial by the Sanhedrin. Early in the morning he was handed over to Pilate. The Sanhedrin could condemn Jesus to die, but only Roman authorities could execute him. The Sanhedrin had to appeal to the Roman authorities to carry out the execution they had decided on. But the charges they had trumped up against Jesus would never stand up before Pilate, so just before turning Jesus over, the Sanhedrin met quickly to fabricate some new legal charges that would hold up (Mark 15:1–4; Luke 23:1–2). They accused Jesus of encouraging tax evasion by telling people not to pay their taxes to Rome; treason, claiming he was a king; and terrorism, causing riots all over the countryside. Blasphemy would mean little to Pilate, but these charges would cause him great concern.

Pilate wasn't all that interested in justice and what was right; he was more concerned with expediency. When he discovered that Jesus was innocent, he actually tried to release him. But he also wanted to try to please the Jewish religious leaders. He went looking for a compromise that would please all sides. Pilate put himself in a no-win situation. He was also getting little cooperation from Jesus. Pilate couldn't believe that Jesus would not defend himself in the midst of the charges being leveled (Matt. 27; Mark 15; John 18).

Finally, Pilate realized that he had to make a decision as to what he was going to do with Jesus Christ, just as, ultimately, each of us must also decide what we will do with Jesus. That's when Pilate came up with an idea to get himself out of this dilemma. Because it was customary to release a prisoner at Passover time, he decided to offer Jesus to the people. But Pilate's plan backfired; the people asked for Barabbas. Pilate couldn't believe what was happening. Barabbas was guilty of murder and leading an insurrection. He was supposed to be crucified with some other criminals. Jesus was innocent and Pilate knew it. He was so shocked at the people's desire to have this chief prisoner of the day released that he asked the crowd what he should do with Jesus. They repeatedly responded, "Crucify him!" (Matt. 27; Luke 23; Mark 15; John 18).

The Jewish leaders wanted Jesus to die on a cross because they believed that this method of death carried with it a curse from God. They got this idea from Deuteronomy 21:23, where it says "anyone hanging on a tree is cursed of God" (TLB). Ultimately, these leaders hoped to convince the people that Jesus was not blessed by God, that he was actually cursed.

Wanting to satisfy the crowd, Pilate released Barabbas and handed Jesus over to be beaten and then crucified (Mark 15:15). Isn't it amazing, centuries later, some still find themselves in the position of wanting to please people instead of God? An innocent man was about to die. However, he was dying in place of the guilty, for you and me.

THE BEATING OF JESUS

Any time a criminal was to be crucified, he was handed over to the elite government soldiers of the day. They were tough, barbaric, and could do whatever they wanted with the prisoner. Jesus was tortured and beaten mercilessly. Then came the humiliation as the soldiers placed a staff in his hand, a purple robe on his back, and a crown of thorns on his head. They began to mock him by kneeling and chanting, "Hail, King of the Jews!" Matthew 27:30 tells us that this company of soldiers then spit on Jesus and repeatedly beat the crown of thorns into his head with the staff. Many people did not survive the soldiers' beatings, but Jesus still had to face the cross. Jesus endured all this because he took our place on the cross to pay our sin debt.

After the illegal all-night trial, followed by an inhuman morning of torture, Jesus was finally led out to be crucified. Beaten and exhausted, he was about to face the most torture-filled death in human history. In accordance with Roman custom, he was forced to carry his cross to the site of the crucifixion as a final act of humiliation. Today scholars and archaeologists disagree over the exact path that Jesus took to his crucifixion. Most agree with the endpoint, identified by the Church of the Holy Sepulcher. The argument is over where Jesus began his walk. The traditionally accepted path—Via Dolorosa, or the Way of Sorrows—is a half-mile stretch running east to west in the Old City, through crowded alleys. However, by arguing over the exact route that Jesus walked, we miss the point of what was accomplished once he got to the site of the crucifixion. It is not important to know the path. We must recognize that he hung on a cross in our place as the remedy for our spiritually terminal disease—sin. It is a disease that is much worse than cancer or AIDS because it will claim every single person unless we respond to God's solution. We must trust Jesus as our Lord and Savior.

THE CRUCIFIXION

Today the cross has been reduced by many people to a piece of ornamental jewelry worn on a chain around the neck. A lot of heavy-metal musicians wear it as part of their stage costume but also include it in the artwork of their CD covers. In the ancient world, the cross was the symbol of execution by crucifixion. For Christians, the cross is not only a symbol of the horrible death of Jesus but also of his triumphant resurrection and the promise of eternal life to all who believe. Let's continue to confront the cross by examining the crucifixion of Jesus.

Shortly after he began his walk to Calvary (Golgotha, "the place of the Skull"), where he was to be crucified, Jesus collapsed under the strain of carrying the cross. Luke 23:26 tells us that Simon from Cyrene (North Africa) was picked out of the crowd to help carry Jesus' cross. As Jesus continued his walk to Calvary, Luke 23 tells of people weeping and exhibiting pity for him in the streets. Jesus stopped just long enough to give people the proper perspective. In essence he said to the crowds, "Don't cry for me, but instead cry for yourselves. Have pity for those who will reject what I am about to do for them." Jesus didn't need the compassion of the crowd. He was facing death on the cross with dignity, honor, and love. The same holds true today. Jesus doesn't want our sympathy; rather he wants our faith and our obedience.

Shortly after Jesus arrived at Golgotha, he was crucified. But he was first offered a wine drink mixed with myrrh, a drug, meant to help deaden the pain of the awful ordeal of those about to die on a cross. The Bible says that Jesus refused this drink. I believe this was because he wanted to be fully coherent on the cross as he took the punishment for our sins.

The crucifixion wasn't pretty, and the Bible gives us few details. The Gospel writers do not record the details of this horror, only the incidents surrounding the crucifixion. However, we can learn much from Roman history. The cross was laid out on the ground and Jesus, being stripped of his clothing, was stretched out on top of it. His hands were nailed to the cross first, after each arm was extended outward from his shoulders. The soldiers found the spot on his wrists where the two bones come together, the spot where you can feel your pulse. Long metal spikes were then driven through his wrists and into the wood.

Nailing his feet to the cross was a more delicate operation. The soldiers crossed one leg over the other. Then they made sure that Jesus' knees were bent. This was done to give the person being crucified the ability to force air into their lungs by stretching their legs up and down. One long spike was then driven through the feet, and the cross was dropped into a hole in the ground. Just imagine the physical agony that Jesus was going through by this time—the pain, the swelling, and add to that the flies now swarming around his open wounds.

Mark 15:25 tells us it was the third hour, or nine o'clock in the morning, when Jesus was crucified. On a sign placed above his head was the charge for which he was being crucified: "King of the Jews." It was a peculiar statement in that it was a true statement, but not in the way the authorities meant it. Jesus offered himself to the Jews and was rejected. Jesus was crucified with two thieves, one on either side of him. This was a fulfillment of the prophecy in Isaiah 53:12: "and [he] was numbered with the transgressors." In Luke 23 (vv. 39–41), we read that one of the criminals hurled insults at Jesus. He mocked Jesus, saying, "If you are who you say you are, why don't you save yourself and us!" However, the other criminal rebuked his buddy by saying, "We did the crime and deserve the punishment, but this man hasn't done anything wrong." This same man then turned to Jesus and said, "Please remember me when you come into your kingdom." Jesus responded, "I tell you the truth, today you will be with me in paradise" (vv. 42–43).

The response of Jesus to this thief is a great reminder of the simple faith that is necessary for us to become members of God's family and to receive his free gift of eternal life. This second thief had no time to clean up his life. He only had time to believe in Jesus. It is not about church membership, good works, or being a moral person. It's about recognizing God's remedy for the sin problem that has separated us from him and why we must receive Christ by personal invitation. Forgiveness of sins and eternal life is given to anyone who believes in Jesus. Faith alone in Christ determines our eternal destiny.

- "Everyone who calls on the name of the Lord will be saved" (Rom. 10:13).
- "For it is by grace you have been saved, through faith—and this not from yourselves, it is the gift of God—not by works, so that no one can boast" (Eph. 2:8–9). (See also John 3:16–18; Acts 16:31; Rom. 4:5).

If we sincerely ask Christ to come into our lives, he will. That's all God has ever asked any sinner to do. God asks us to come to him in simple and humble faith. Then we are born into God's family through the supernatural work of the Holy Spirit. This is great news that needs to be shared with everyone we know!

Remember, Jesus could have chosen to save himself. He could have instantly killed those who mocked him and nailed him to that cross. Instead, Jesus endured the suffering and shame of the cross because of his great love for us. Jesus paid a tremendous price to free us from the penalty of sin. In 1 Peter 2:24 we read: "He himself bore our sins in his body on the tree, so that we might die to sins and live for righteousness; by his wounds you have been healed." Just think, because Jesus died our death and paid the penalty on the cross for our sin, we were actually part of the events that took place that day. Therefore, the only possible way for us to respond to this ultimate act of sacrificial love is to acknowledge our need as sinners—separated from God—and freely receive his forgiveness.

In his Gospel, Mark continues to give a report of the crucifixion, by the hour, with verse 15:33: "At the sixth hour darkness came over the whole land until the ninth hour." Just imagine, from twelve noon until three o'clock the sun's light was gone. In darkness, hanging on the cross, Jesus paid the penalty for our sins and bridged the gap between a holy God and a sinful people. The prophet Isaiah writes: "Surely he took up our infirmities and carried our sorrows, yet we considered him stricken by God, smitten by him, and afflicted. But he was pierced for our transgressions, he was crushed for our iniquities: the punishment that brought us peace was upon him, and by his wounds we are healed" (53:4–5). For the first and only time in all eternity, God turned his back on Jesus and punished him for the sins of the human race. Jesus was rejected so we could be accepted.

According to Luke 23:46, at the ninth hour Jesus called out in a loud voice, "Father, into your hands I commit my spirit." John 19 adds that Jesus said he was thirsty and asked for a drink. He was given a drink from a sponge soaked in wine vinegar and then said, "'It is finished.' With that, he bowed his head and gave up his spirit" (v. 30). He did not die because his body stopped functioning; instead, he surrendered up his spirit. He died differently than anyone else ever did. He accomplished everything that was needed for us to receive and experience God's grace. That's why Jesus could say with confidence, "It is finished." What was a cry of agony from Jesus became a cry of victory for us.

Jesus had confidence and perfect peace as he placed his spirit in the Father's hands. Do you have enough peace and trust to place your life in the Father's hands? How about your future? Your marriage? Your children? Your finances? God wants us to surrender every dimension of our lives to him when we become part of his forever family. We can rest assured that God will take care of us since we know the tremendous sacrifice that was made on our behalf.

THE BURIAL

Because Jesus died a few hours before sundown at the beginning of the Sabbath, something had to be done with his body. It was not only against Jewish law to do work or travel on the Sabbath; it was also against Jewish law to allow a dead body to remain exposed overnight. The end of the Sabbath was at sundown Saturday; therefore, something had to be done quickly with the body of Jesus.

After Jesus died, Joseph of Arimathea went to Pilate and asked for Jesus' body. Even though Joseph was a member of the Sanhedrin, he was also a little-known follower of Jesus. Joseph boldly stepped out to take charge of Jesus' burial when the apostles had scattered and gone into hiding. Because of his position as an honored member of the Jewish "Supreme Court," Joseph risked his reputation to give proper burial to the one he had secretly followed. It is never easy to risk your reputation, even if it is for something that is right. Next time you feel intimidated at taking a stand for your faith when your reputation is at stake, remember Joseph and all that he stood to lose when he risked his reputation to properly bury Jesus.

Pilate was surprised that Jesus had died so quickly (Mark 15:42–44). He even asked a soldier to make absolutely certain that Jesus was in fact dead. Typically a person who was crucified could linger alive on the cross for days. Their life would gradually expire after this cruel mode of torture. Usually a prisoner's death on a cross could be speeded up by breaking his legs. In the case of Jesus, this was not necessary because he was already dead. This fulfilled the prophecy that not a single bone in his body would be broken.

Joseph, who was a wealthy man, bought fine linen cloth, wrapped the body in it, and placed Jesus in his own burial tomb. This tomb was probably cut out of a large rock, with space big enough to stand in. A huge stone was then rolled across the door of the tomb (Mark 15:46). Matthew 27:66 also tells us that it was sealed by the Roman authorities and Roman guards were posted. The death of Christ was witnessed and confirmed by many—including the soldier, Pilate, the religious leaders, Joseph, and the women.

Why did Jesus have to die? The full meaning of the death of Christ cannot possibly be captured in one chapter. However, we can highlight some of the results of the death of Christ in such a way as to gain more practical insight into all that was accomplished on our behalf. Matthew 20:28 tells us that "the Son of Man did not come to be served, but to serve, and to give his life as a ransom for many." This verse lays the foundation for why Jesus had to die on the cross.

First, according to 2 Corinthians 5:21 and 1 Peter 3:18, by dying on a Roman cross Jesus died as a substitute for the whole human race. The demands of a holy, righteous God were completely met through Christ's death on the cross. His payment for sin was total and complete. It is because of Christ's substitutionary death that God may declare us righteous and adopt us into his family without compromising his holiness. Every one of our sins was placed on Jesus, who completely settled the score and paid for them through his death on the cross.

A second important result of the death of Christ is redemption. This truth is stated in 1 Corinthians 6:20 where we learn that as believers we have been "bought with a price" (KJV). The concept of being bought is that of a slave being purchased in the ancient public slave market. Jesus bought us out of the "slave market of sin" and set us free (see 1 Cor. 7:23; Gal. 3:13; 4:5; Rev. 5:9). We are not only redeemed from the slavery of sin; we are redeemed by the payment of Christ's blood shed on the cross, and ultimately we are redeemed to a condition of freedom by which we serve the Lord because of what he has done for us.

The third result of Christ's death on the cross is that all of humanity is reconciled with God. Because of the rebellion that took place in the Garden of Eden by Adam and Eve, we were alienated and estranged from God. We were enemies of God. Our sin moved us out of fellowship with God, and Christ's death was the only way for us to have this relationship restored. Reconciliation is when God restores man to a proper relationship with himself and establishes peace where there was previously hatred and hostility (see 2 Cor. 5:18–20). The death of Christ forever changes our state of being an enemy into one of being in complete harmony with the living God.

Moreover, the death of Christ fully satisfied all the demands of a holy God. This is called *propitiation*. God is holy and cannot have a relationship with sinful people. He has a divine hostility toward sin, in a personal way. Appeasing God's wrath was not a matter of vengeance but one of justice. This justice could only be satisfied in one way: through the sacrificial gift of God's only Son. Romans 3:25 teaches that Christ provided a satisfactory payment for sin through his death on the cross. Ultimately, God's wrath was diverted and his holiness was not compromised because his demands were fully satisfied through the death of Christ.

Christ's death likewise resulted in forgiveness for sinners. In order to forgive sin, God had to have proper payment. The death of Jesus provided the legal means by which God could forgive sin. According to Colossians 2:13, God has made us alive in Christ and forgives us all our sins. Jesus took all of our sins upon himself so that we could have a new life. God forgives us out of grace and sends our sins away (Matt. 6:12, 9:6; James 5:15; 1 John 1:9). Corrie Ten Boom, whose life inspired the book and movie *The Hiding Place,* said, "God takes our sin and throws it to the bottom of the sea and puts up a big sign that says 'No fishing.'" What a great word picture! Because of Christ's death on the cross, we are totally and completely forgiven.

Another result of the death of Christ is justification, or the legal act by which God the judge declares the believing sinner to be righteous. In Romans 5:1 we learn, "Therefore, since we have been justified through faith, we have peace with God through our Lord Jesus Christ." Because of the price Christ paid by his death on the cross, there is no more hostility between us and God. There is no sin hindering our relationship with him. This concept of justification has two sides to it: first is the aspect of having our sins removed; second is the aspect of the righteousness of Christ being granted to the life of the believer.

God was completely satisfied because of Christ's death on the cross. Since this is the case, then what can we as sinners do to try and appease God? Absolutely nothing. God has taken care of everything himself. We only need to receive the gift of love and forgiveness that God offers.

Ultimately, Jesus died so we could be forgiven and have a brand-new life and a fresh power for living. The cross of Christ is the only hope we have in a world that is confused and lost.

RESPONDING TO THE CROSS

When we look at the cross of Christ, we should do so in awe and gratitude as we realize all that he did for us. Jesus paid a tremendous price to free us from the penalty of sin. Because God is loving, holy, merciful, patient, and full of grace, our lives can be radically changed.

If you are a follower of Christ, the quality of your life should be different because of the transformation that has taken place as a result of Christ's work on the cross. Your life should be characterized by power, love, and victory over temptation. Jesus did not go through the agony of the cross for us to live frustrated, empty, and unproductive lives.

Easter is about peace, hope, and new life. Nothing is more important than knowing the Jesus of Easter personally and having his resurrection power be a reality in your life. The cross of Christ not only shows us the love of God; moreover, it gives us a new power for life and a guarantee of eternal life. If you do not yet have the hope that Christ brings, please continue to read what Easter is all about and how you too can find eternal life.

PART 3:

LIVING IN LIGHT OF EASTER

CHAPTER 8

Getting Back to the Heart of Easter

Edith Burns was a wonderful Christian who lived in San Antonio, Texas. She was the patient of Dr. Will Phillips, a gentle doctor who saw patients as people. His favorite patient was Edith Burns.

One morning he went to his office with a heavy heart because of Edith Burns. When he walked into the waiting room, there sat Edith with her big black Bible in her lap, earnestly talking to a young mother sitting beside her. Edith Burns had a habit of introducing herself in this way: "Hello, my name is Edith Burns. Do you believe in Easter?" Then she would explain the meaning of Easter, and many times people would be saved.

Dr. Phillips walked into his office and saw the head nurse, Beverly. She had first met Edith when she was taking Edith's blood pressure. Edith had greeted her by saying, "My name is Edith Burns. Do you believe in Easter?" Beverly said, "Why yes, I do." Edith replied, "Well, what do you believe about Easter?" Beverly answered, "Well, it's all about egg hunts, going to church, and dressing up." Edith kept pressing her about the real meaning of Easter, and finally led her to a saving knowledge of Jesus Christ.

"Beverly, don't call Edith into the office quite yet. I believe there is another delivery taking place in the waiting room," Dr. Phillips explained. Later, after being called back in the doctor's office, Edith sat down, and when she took a look at the doctor, she said, "Dr. Will, why are you so sad? Are you reading your Bible? Are you praying?"

Dr. Phillips said gently, "Edith, I'm the doctor and you're the patient." With a heavy heart he said, "Your lab report came back and it says you have cancer, Edith; you're not going to live very long."

"Why, Will Phillips, shame on you!" she exclaimed. "Why are you so sad? Do you think God makes mistakes? You have just told me I'm going to see my precious Lord Jesus, my husband, and my friends. You have just told me that I am going to celebrate Easter forever, and here you are having difficulty giving me my ticket!" *What a magnificent woman this Edith Burns is!* Dr. Phillips thought to himself.

Edith continued coming to Dr. Phillips. Christmas came, and the office was closed through January 3. On the day the office opened, Edith didn't show up. Later that afternoon, Edith called Dr. Phillips and said she must move her story to the hospital. She said, "Will, I'm very near home, so make sure that they put women next to me in my room who need to know about Easter."

Women began to come in and share that room with Edith. Many women were saved. Everybody on that floor, from staff to patients, was so excited about Edith that they started calling her Edith Easter—everybody except Phyllis Cross, the head nurse.

Phyllis made it plain that she wanted nothing to do with Edith, a "religious nut." She had been a nurse in an army hospital. She had seen it all and heard it all. She was the original G.I. Jane. She had been married three times, and she was hard, cold, and did everything by the book.

One morning the two nurses who were to attend to Edith were sick. Edith had the flu, and Phyllis had to go in and give her a shot. When she walked in, Edith had a big smile on her face and said happily, "Phyllis, God loves you and I love you, and I have been praying for you." Phyllis Cross said, "Well, you can quit praying for me, it won't work. I'm not interested." Edith replied, "Well, I will pray, and I have asked God not to let me go home until you come into the family." Phyllis Cross answered, "Then you will never die because that will never happen," and curtly walked out of the room.

Every day Phyllis would walk into the room, and Edith would say, "God loves you, Phyllis, and I love you, and I'm praying for you." One day, Phyllis Cross said she was literally drawn to Edith's room, like a magnet draws iron. She sat down on the bed and Edith whispered, "I'm so glad you have come because God told me that today is your special day."

Phyllis said, "Edith, you have asked everybody here the question, 'Do you believe in Easter?' but you have never asked me." "Phyllis," Edith answered, "I wanted to many times, but God told me to wait until you asked, and now that you have asked . . . ."

Edith Burns took her Bible and shared with Phyllis Cross the Easter story of the death, burial, and resurrection of Jesus Christ. Edith said, "Phyllis, do you believe in Easter? Do you believe that Jesus Christ is alive and that he wants to live in your heart?" Phyllis Cross replied, "Oh, I want to believe that with all of my heart, and I do want Jesus in my life." Right there, Phyllis prayed and invited Jesus Christ into her heart. For the first time, Phyllis didn't walk out of a hospital room; she was carried out on the wings of angels.

Two days later, Phyllis came in and Edith said, "Do you know what day it is?" Phyllis answered, "Why Edith, it's Good Friday." Edith said, "Oh, no. For you, every day is Easter. Happy Easter, Phyllis!"

Two days later, on Easter Sunday, Phyllis Cross came into work, did some of her duties, and then went down to the flower shop and got some Easter lilies. She wanted to go up to see Edith and give her some Easter lilies and wish her a happy Easter. When she walked into Edith's room, Edith was in bed. That big black Bible was on her lap. Her hands were in that Bible. There was a sweet smile on her face. When Phyllis went to pick up Edith's hand, she realized Edith was dead. Her left hand was on John 14:2–3: "In my Father's house are many mansions. . . . I go to prepare a place for you. . . . I will come again and receive you unto myself; that where I am, there you may be also" (KJV). Her right hand was on Revelation 21:4, "And God will wipe away every tear from their eyes; and there shall be no more death, neither sorrow, nor crying; and neither shall there be any more pain: for the former things are passed away" (KJV). Phyllis Cross took one look at that dead body, and then lifted her face toward heaven, and with tears streaming down her cheeks, said, "Happy Easter, Edith. Happy Easter!"

Phyllis Cross left Edith's body and walked out of the room and over to a table where two student nurses were sitting. She said, "My name is Phyllis Cross. Do you believe in Easter?"[5]

DO YOU BELIEVE IN EASTER?

Do you believe in Easter? The story that is told in the Bible? Even though Easter has managed to hang on to its religious significance more than Christmas, many children (and adults) in the United States, and around the world, are confused about its true meaning. They see it as a time to colorfully decorate hard-boiled eggs, wear new clothes, and indulge in candy from the basket that the Easter bunny brought.

Easter should be the most exciting time of year for a Christian. Yet a darkening anxiety can easily enshroud our celebration. In households everywhere, we worry that our best efforts at orchestrating the holiday events will fall short, and we realize too late that we have lost our focus. What happened to Jesus?

Many people today are looking for a way to leave this holiday treadmill. Can you relate? Do you ever find yourself with similar feelings at Easter? There are healthy alternatives to this stress-filled ritual, better ways to celebrate the greatest event in history. However, you must determine that it is time for a change and then develop a plan to make the necessary changes to establish a balance that is both fun and appropriate for your family. And it's best to put this plan together early in the spring so as not to be swept away in the all-too-typical holiday confusion.

Let's take a look at some practical examples of what we can do to get back to the heart of Easter.

FAMILY TRADITIONS

Developing special traditions is an important element for healthy families. Easter is a great time to acquire fun and meaningful holiday practices that will provide fond memories in the lives of parents and kids alike. With such a highly mobile society and the fracturing of so many families today, special traditions can help give children a sense of security as they look forward to certain practices each holiday season. These traditions can also help deepen their faith from a practical aspect, as they have the opportunity to celebrate the resurrection of Christ in a variety of different ways.

Ever since our twins were old enough to remember things, my wife and I have made an effort to form meaningful traditions for our family at Easter time. And now our youngest daughter is also sharing in these family practices. Here's a rundown of some of the Russo Easter traditions we practice each year that help to keep our family focused on our Savior's triumph over death. Maybe these will give you some ideas of things that your family might be able to do.

Bake Special Easter Cookies

Here's a recipe for cookies to be baked on the night before Easter. As you mix the ingredients and bake the cookies, you will also be highlighting key elements of the Easter story.

Ingredients	
1 cup whole pecans	1 cup sugar
1 tsp. vinegar	Ziplock bag
3 egg whites	Wooden spoon
Pinch of salt	Tape
	Bible

Preheat oven to 300 degrees Fahrenheit. This is important to do first; don't wait until you're halfway done with the recipe.

Place pecans in Ziplock bag and let children beat them with the wooden spoon to break nuts into little pieces. Explain that after Jesus was arrested, he was beaten by Roman soldiers. Read John 19:1–3.

Let each child smell the vinegar. Put 1 teaspoon into a mixing bowl. Illustrate that when Jesus hung on the cross, he was given vinegar to drink. Read John 19:28–30.

Add the egg whites to the vinegar. Eggs represent life. Explain that Jesus gave his life to give us abundant and eternal life. Read John 10:10–11.

Sprinkle a little salt into each child's hand. Let them taste it, then brush the rest of it into the bowl. Illustrate that this represents the salty tears shed by the followers of Jesus. It also represents the bitterness of our own sin. Read Luke 23:27.

So far, the ingredients have not been very mouth-watering. Now it's time to change that.

Add one cup of sugar. Explain that the sweetest part of the story is that Jesus died, in our place, on the cross because he loves us. He wants us to know him intimately and be a part of his forever family. Read Psalm 34:8 and John 3:16.

Beat ingredients in bowl on high speed for twelve to fifteen minutes until stiff peaks form. Explain that the color white represents the purity in God's eyes of those whose sins have been forgiven (cleansed) by Jesus. Our sins become "white as snow" as we are born again. Read Isaiah 1:18 and John 3:1–3.

Fold in the broken pecan nuts. Drop dough by teaspoons onto wax paper-covered cookie sheets. Explain that each mound represents the rocky tomb where Jesus' body was placed. Read Matthew 27:57–60.

Put the cookie sheets in the oven, close the door, and turn the oven OFF. Give each child a piece of tape and seal the oven door. Explain that Jesus' tomb was sealed. Read Matthew 27:65–66. Send the kids off to bed, but first explain to them that they may feel sad by leaving the cookies in the oven overnight. This is the same way that Jesus' followers felt when the tomb was sealed. Read John 16:20–22.

On Easter morning, open the oven and give everyone a cookie. Notice how the surface of the cookie is cracked, and then take a bite. The cookies are hollow! On the first Easter Sunday morning, Jesus' followers were amazed to find the stone rolled away and the tomb empty. Read Matthew 28:1–9.

ATTEND AN EASTER PLAY

Many churches in southern California have special Easter events open to the public. The Crystal Cathedral presents a magnificent production called "The Glory of Easter." It is an all-encompassing event that utilizes drama, music, and live animals.

STUDY ETHNIC TRADITIONS

On a more serious note, have you looked into some of the Easter holiday traditions of your own ethnic heritage? Not only can these be fun for your family to participate in, but they can also give your children a sense of "roots" in an oftentimes insecure world. In addition, learning more about their heritage can help build their sense of identity. Ultimately, security, significance, and acceptance—for kids and adults—can only be found in the Jesus of Easter.

READ EASTER BOOKS

Our family also enjoys reading a variety of books and short stories together during the holiday season. There are a number of good Easter books and stories that are great for all ages to enjoy. We have provided a few fun things to read together as well as a short suggested book list in the appendix of this book.

USE A FAMILY DEVOTIONAL
"The Twelve Days of Easter"

This devotional is designed to help you and your family focus on the heart of Easter and how it affects every aspect of the Christian life. The Easter basket and eggs are meant to be used year after year as you continue this special family tradition.

Items You Will Need

A straw or plastic basket

Twelve plastic eggs, numbered one through twelve. Place the following items inside the corresponding numbered egg:

1. A small piece of bread
2. A coin (nickel, dime, or quarter)
3. A small strand of rope or heavy twine
4. A piece of purple-colored cloth
5. A small piece of a rosebush branch, including at least one thorn, or a toothpick
6. A miniature cross, preferably a wooden one
7. A small nail
8. A tiny piece of sponge
9. A miniature spear or sword (a small plastic one, often found on cheese and vegetable trays)
10. On a small piece of cardboard write the following words: Jesus of Nazareth, the King of the Jews
11. A stone, preferably a smooth, flat one
12. Keep this egg empty to signify the empty tomb

What to Do

Set aside time each day during the twelve days preceding Easter to get your family together for a special time of Bible study and discussion. Your time together will center around the twelve plastic eggs. Because each egg is numbered, you will know which one to open on a given day.

Remember to read the Scripture verse for that day before opening the egg. Depending upon the ages of your children, have a different child read the verse each day. Make sure that you take time to guess what is inside the egg, based on the verse, before opening it. Then, as a family discuss the significance of that item and how it relates to the Easter story. Close each day's devotional with a time of prayer.

Day One. The time of the Feast of the Unleavened Bread had arrived. The Passover lamb was now ready to be sacrificed. Jesus, along with his disciples, was preparing for the Last Supper. Read Luke 22:7–19.

For the clue to the first egg, read verse 19 again. What do you think is in the first egg?

After a brief time of discussion, pray together.

Day Two. The chief priests and teachers of the law (the religious leaders) were looking for a way to get rid of Jesus with the Passover fast approaching. They finally found a way. Read Luke 22:1–5.

For your clue to the second egg, read Matthew 26:14–15. What's inside the egg?

After a brief time of discussion, pray together.

Day Three. Jesus had been betrayed by a friend. He was arrested and taken before the Sanhedrin—the Court of Justice or Supreme Jewish Court. Read Matthew 26:57–67.

To get a clue for your next egg, read Matthew 27:2. What do you think is in this egg?

After a brief time of discussion, pray together.

Day Four. The soldiers made fun of Jesus. They mocked and insulted him. Read Luke 22:63–65.

Your "egg" clue will be found in Matthew 27:28. Open egg four to see if you guessed right.

After a brief time of discussion, pray together.

Day Five. Jesus suffered quite a bit at the hands of his enemies. Read Matthew 27:27–31.

This next egg's clue is found in Matthew 27:29.

Note: The crown of thorns was meant to be a symbol that made fun of royalty. This crown was woven out of a rough bush with thorns that were one to three inches long. After setting the crown on Jesus' head, the soldiers beat it into his scalp.

After a brief time of discussion, pray together.

Day Six. Each year during Passover, the governor would free one person from prison. This prisoner was always someone the people wanted to see set free. This year there was a man named Barabbas who was in jail the same time as Jesus. He was a bad man and deserved to be in prison. Pilate, the governor, gave the people a choice: Did they want Jesus or Barabbas to go free? The crowd chose Barabbas.

Read John 19:16–17. Your clue for the egg will be found in these verses.

After a brief time of discussion, pray together.

Day Seven. Pilate tried everything he could think of to set Jesus free. But the people said that if Pilate let Jesus go, they would not be a friend of Caesar, the Roman king at that time.

Read John 19:12–15. Your clue will be found in John 19:15. If you can't figure it out, look at John 20:25.

After a brief time of discussion, pray together.

Day Eight. Jesus died on a cross. This was a terrible way to die. Read John 19:28–29.

Why do you think people gave Jesus vinegar instead of water to drink?

In biblical times vinegar was a fermented acidic drink that was enjoyed by laborers in wine-growing countries. The Romans had a similar drink that was part of a soldier's food rations.

What is in egg number eight? For your clue read John 19:29.

After a brief time of discussion, pray together.

Day Nine. Right after Jesus received the vinegar drink, he said, "It is finished!" Then he put his head down and died. Read John 19:31–37.

What's in this egg? The clue is found in verse 34.

After a brief time of discussion, pray together.

Day Ten. A sign was placed above Jesus' head. This sign had a very special message printed on it. Read John 19:19.

Did you guess what's in the egg? Open it to see if you were right.

After a brief time of discussion, pray together.

Day Eleven. After Jesus died, the Pharisees were afraid that some of the disciples would try and steal his body and say that Jesus had risen from the dead. Read Matthew 27:62–63 and 28:2.

The clue for what's found in the egg is in Matthew 27:66.

After a brief time of discussion, pray together.

Day Twelve. He is risen! God raised him from the grave. Jesus is alive! When Jesus rose again, he defeated Satan and death. Read Matthew 28:1–10.

This last egg is a special one. It represents an awesome promise for every believer in Christ. Discuss this idea and why it offers hope for us.

After a brief time of discussion, pray together.

An alternative to making your own eggs is to purchase FamilyLife's Resurrection Eggs.® Their creativity and simplicity help boys and girls understand their need for a Savior. The twelve colorful eggs—containing miniature objects illustrating the death, burial, and resurrection of Jesus—will captivate the children you love. (Resurrection Eggs® are sold at most Christian retail stores or are available from FamilyLife by calling 1-800-FL-TODAY or going online at www.familylife.com.)

Have a Family Film Festival

As a family, we have also established the tradition of watching our collection of Easter videos each year. We start around the beginning of Lent and go through an assortment of classics, including animated films and the time-honored "The Ten Commandments." This has become a fun time for our family to relax and be together. These films also provide a basis for some interesting discussions on what each film actually says about Easter. Some contain strong underlying Christian themes. Other suggested videos include the *Jesus Video*—both the regular version and the children's version—and the Visual Bible Topical Series *The Passion—The Last Days of Christ*. A host of animated children's videos can be found in any local Christian bookstore.

Celebrate the Passover Meal (Seder)

This is a new tradition in the Russo household that we participate in on Good Friday evening. Passover is known by a couple of names: "Festival of Freedom" or "Feast of Unleavened Bread." It commemorates the freedom from slavery and exodus of the Jews from ancient Egypt.

A highlight of Passover is the "Seder," a ritual meal traditionally served in the home. The Passover story is told, special foods are eaten, select Scripture passages are read, and time is spent in prayer as a family. A very large "Seder Plate" is placed in the center of the table. This serving plate contains the symbolic foods of Passover.

- Fresh greens (as a symbol of springtime and rebirth)
- Bitter herbs (such as romaine lettuce and parsley, a reminder of the bitterness of slavery)
- Horseradish (another reminder of the bitterness of slavery)
- Hard-boiled eggs (a reminder of ancient festival offerings in Jerusalem)
- *Haroset* (use a mixture of applesauce, nuts, and cinnamon; symbolizes the mortar used by Jewish slaves to build Egyptian temples and cities)
- Roasted lamb shank (representing the lamb sacrificed at the first Passover)

Next to the Seder plate place a bowl of salt water, for dipping vegetables, and three pieces of *matzo* (flat crackerlike bread) covered with a special cloth.

Other favorite dishes that can be served for the meal are:

• chicken	• carrots
• brisket	• chicken soup with matzo balls
• turkey	• angel food cake
• chopped fish	• Passover cake made with honey
• potatoes	• macaroons

The meal is supposed to be eaten in a reclining position as a reminder of the "comforts of freedom." In some cases you can place a cushion on everyone's left side to help facilitate this; however, it's not a necessity to experience a meaningful Seder. During the meal, adults traditionally drink four glasses of wine to celebrate the promises God made to Moses: that God would bring the Jews out of Egypt and deliver them from slavery, and then make them a nation. Sparkling grape or apple juice can be substituted for the wine.

Traditionally there is also to be an extra plate set for the prophet Elijah. The Jews believe he will eventually come to declare peace among all the people of the world. His glass is filled and left untouched throughout the meal. After the meal, the front door is opened so that Elijah may enter.

After arranging the table and the food for the meal, the candles need to be lit. Light one for the light of salvation (read Ps. 27:1); a second for God's Word is light (read Ps. 119:105); and a third one for the Word being God (read John. 1:1–5). Now it's time to begin the fourteen traditional steps of the Seder. I have changed each step slightly, adding Scripture and brief explanations where appropriate, in light of the fact that as Christians we know that the Messiah has come. This does not take away from the meaning of this special meal and should only prove to enhance your family's observance of the Seder.

1. The first cup of wine is blessed. Read Exodus 6:1; Psalm 24:3–4.

2. Everyone has their hands washed (premoistened towlettes work well here). Read Psalm 24:3–4; John 13:5, 12–14.

3. The vegetable is dipped in the salt water. The green vegetable is a reminder of life rejuvenated, and the salt water is "life immersed in tears." Read Exodus 1:12–14.

4. The middle piece of *matzo* is broken, wrapped in the special cloth, and hidden somewhere in the house. The broken matzo reminds us that Christ's body was broken and bruised for our sin. Read Isaiah 53:5 and Zechariah 12:10. The hidden piece of matzo is also a symbol of Christ's body being "hidden away" in the tomb. This hidden piece of bread is called the *afikomen*.

5. The Passover story is told. Here's one version that can be used.

> More than three thousand years ago, a cruel Pharaoh came into power in Egypt and forced the Jews into a life of slavery. Pharaoh ordered every male child of the Jews to be killed. A special baby boy was saved because his mother floated him down a river in a basket. The baby was found by Pharaoh's daughter and raised as an Egyptian prince. He was given the name Moses.

Many years later, God told Moses to ask Pharaoh to release his people from slavery. Because Pharaoh didn't listen, God punished the Egyptians with ten plagues. The final plague brought death to the first-born of every Egyptian household. In order for the angel of death to "pass over" the Jewish homes, Moses instructed the Jews to paint their doors with the blood of a sacrificed lamb.

Pharaoh finally freed the slaves after his own son died. The Jews left Egypt so quickly that they didn't even wait for their bread to rise. But Pharaoh's anger consumed him and he sent Egyptian soldiers to pursue the Jews in their escape. When they reached the Red Sea, it parted for the Jews and destroyed the soldiers.

Four questions are asked and briefly discussed at this time:

A. On all the other nights we eat bread that rises. Why do we only eat unleavened bread tonight? (It is a symbol of fleeing Egypt and the bread of affliction.)

B. On all other nights we eat all kinds of vegetables. Why do we eat only bitter herbs tonight? (It is a reminder of the life of slavery the Jews endured in Egypt.)

C. On all other nights we do not dip the vegetables even once. Why do we dip them twice tonight? (Jesus gave Judas a way out, and we have all betrayed Jesus.)

D. On all other nights we eat our meals sitting or standing. On this night why do we recline? (After safely fleeing Egypt, the Israelites could finally rest in the desert. You can also read Matt. 11:28.)

The second cup of wine is now blessed and drunk.

6. All hands are washed before the meal.
7. Blessings are said over the matzo.
8. The bitter herbs are tasted and then dipped in the *haroset*.
9. A matzo and bitter herb sandwich is eaten.

10. The main meal is eaten.

11. Children search for the *afikomen*. The one who finds it gets a prize.

12. Blessings are sung after the meal, and the third cup of wine is drunk. The door is opened for Elijah. (Singing does not work for every family. You may want to play a favorite praise CD, and those who feel comfortable can sing along with one song. Or simply have a time of prayer.)

13. Sing psalms (once again you can use a CD). The fourth cup of wine is drunk.

14. Traditional songs are sung. What are some of your family's favorite praise and worship songs? Or you can make use of a CD. Close with the Passover wish: "Next year I will see you in Jerusalem!" Then read Psalms 113–118.

The objective in serving a Passover meal for your family is not to become so strict in following the ritual that it becomes burdensome for you. The idea is to do something to bring a deeper meaning to your celebration of Easter and to develop new traditions for your family to observe each year.

As you can see, we have found a multitude of things to do as a family during the Easter season. Some things are just for fun and others allow for spiritual input. You are only limited by time and imagination. By making a concerted effort, each activity can become part of a family tradition and offer another opportunity to celebrate the resurrection of Jesus Christ.

TELLING OTHERS THE GREAT NEWS

There is no better time to tell others the great news about Jesus than at Easter. Many people seem to be more receptive to spiritual talk, while others are desperately searching for ways to overcome their pain and loneliness.

The apostle Paul reminds us in 2 Corinthians 5:20 that we are "Christ's ambassadors." Easter offers us numerous opportunities to fulfill this biblical responsibility in our family, on our campus, in our neighborhood, on the job, and in the world. We should approach the Easter season with prayerful attention to those we may come in contact with who need to establish a relationship with Jesus. Then carefully and thoughtfully share the message of Easter with them. This can take place in a variety of ways, from inviting someone to a special Easter service, to taking a few extra minutes to share one-on-one how Easter has changed your life. Sometimes these opportunities come to us personally. Other times the Lord opens doors for us to take the message of Easter to others in different situations and through a variety of organizations. In each case we are sharing the greatest news ever: Jesus is alive!

At our home church, Pomona First Baptist, we have a couple of ways to reach out to others with a message of Easter hope. Every Easter Sunday morning, we have a service at the Los Angeles County Fairgrounds grandstand. When people arrive, they are treated to fresh Krispy Kreme donuts and coffee. As families head into the grandstand to get a seat, children are given an activity packet that includes a small stuffed animal. There is lots of great music and a relevant Easter message from our pastor, Glen Gunderson. This is a great, nonthreatening place to bring unsaved relatives and friends to hear the true message of Easter.

Many churches offer special services and activities on Easter Sunday morning. A friend of mine is the pastor of Twin Lakes Church in Aptos, California, where they have added a unique touch on Easter for unchurched people. Besides refreshments served between services, they have a petting zoo for families to enjoy, with lots of tiny animals. The church also offers free family portrait pictures. Since Easter is one of the traditional Sundays in the year for families to attend church, this is a nice touch for them. Once again, the church offers lots of great music and a timely message from my friend, Pastor Rene Schlaepfer.

Another way our home church encourages reaching out to others at Easter is through Easter food baskets. This is a great way to show the love of God at Easter to those who are less fortunate. People in the church are encouraged to donate money to purchase gift certificates or give specific items for the baskets (canned fruit, biscuit/pancake mix, canned tuna or meats, boxed potatoes or pasta, flour, canned juices and soups, oil/shortening, paper good items, etc.). These baskets are then distributed to needy families in the church and community. This is also something your family could do personally for a family that you know is in need.

WHY CELEBRATE EASTER?

It is easy to get caught up in the commercialism that clouds our understanding of Easter. Losing a sense of wonder and excitement as we prepare to commemorate the death, burial, and resurrection of Jesus Christ has become all too routine, even in Christian homes.

Getting back to the heart of Easter is no easy task, especially with so much of our culture barraging us with opposing messages and confusing consumerism. Easter doesn't have to be filled with frenzied activity and weariness. However, to successfully make Easter Christ-centered for you and your family, it will require a commitment to change, and the development of a plan to implement. Let me caution you to work on this plan well before the Easter season hits. It may be too late to make all the changes necessary for this season, but don't put it off until next year. At least begin the process now. Do what you can for this Easter, then determine to continue the process next year.

The Bible gives some practical counsel on getting back to the heart of Easter. Romans 12:2 reads: "Don't become so well-adjusted to your culture that you fit into it without even thinking. Instead, fix your attention on God. You'll be changed from the inside out" (TM). The behavior and customs of our world are often confusing and self-centered. Our refusal to conform to the world must go deeper than just a certain level of behavior. It must be firmly founded in our minds and hearts. Changing from the inside out requires the renewing of our minds. This can only happen when Christ gives us a new attitude. Then we can be transformed and have the ability to not be conformed to the world. The Bible plays a vital role in the rejuvenation of our minds. A steady diet of God's Word is crucial.

As Matthew 6:33 reminds us, we must give God first place in our lives. We must turn to him for help and guidance in every dimension of our lives, including how we celebrate Easter. We must fill our thoughts with his desires, make his character our pattern, and determine to obey him.

It's all up to you. No one else can get back to the heart of Easter for you and your family. It's a choice that you must make, a plan that you and your family must develop. Make sure that no matter what activities your family is involved in during the Easter season, Jesus is the foundation for what is done. Without question, it's worth all the effort it will take. Remember, getting back to the heart of Easter will also help set the pace for keeping Christ in the center of yours and your family's lives the rest of the year.

Above all else, remember the ultimate reason that we celebrate Easter, found in 1 Corinthians 15:13–14: "For if there is no resurrection of the dead, then Christ has not been raised either. And if Christ was not raised, then all our preaching is useless, and your trust in God is useless" (NLT).

CHAPTER 9

Parenting in a Junk-Food Culture

Kids today are filling up on junk food like never before. *Newsweek* magazine ran a cover story entitled, "Fat for Life? Six Million Kids Are Seriously Overweight. What Families Can Do about It." The article points out that new, bigger meals means bigger kids. For example, a traditional McDonald's burger with a 16-ounce Coke and a small order of fries carries 627 calories and 10 grams of fat. Upgrade to a Big Xtra with cheese and "supersize" the drink and fries, and now your lunch packs 1,805 calories and 84 grams of fat. It's no wonder that the percentage of kids who are overweight has more than doubled since the 1960s. In 1991, only four states had obesity rates more than 14 percent. By 1998, 37 had hit that threshold.[6] Welcome to our junk-food culture.

And it's not just junk food for the body that this generation is filling up on. Junk food for the mind is equally menacing. It's available everywhere, from MP3 music to satellite TV to computer games to surfing the World Wide Web. Nowadays mental and emotional junk food is stifling the growth of our kids and fracturing our families.

Life for kids today is a minefield. We have a generation of young people who are consuming things at such a rapid pace that not only are they unaware of what they are devouring, they are also failing to appreciate who they are and all that they possess. Unfortunately, for the average kid and family, Easter is more about chocolate bunnies and marshmallow eggs than the resurrection of Jesus Christ. Cartoonist Bill Keane captured the confusion in "Family Circus" when Billy asks, "Can I wear my Halloween costume for Easter?"[7]

Life is confusing and complex for today's kids, as well as for their parents and grandparents. There is a battle raging for the minds and emotions of our kids. So much is coming at them from so many different directions. They have open, interested minds and soft hearts. Moreover, they are individuals with a tremendous spiritual hunger, seeking help and hope to navigate through the enticements of contemporary culture.

Remembering why we celebrate Easter is an important current issue that demands strong and thoughtful parental guidance. It's not easy being a mom or dad today, and everyone knows that parenting is risky business. There are no money-back guarantees that all will turn out well for our children. However, God does promise us in Proverbs 22:6 that if we "point our kids in the right direction, when they're old, they won't be lost" (TM). The key to raising healthy kids in a junk-food culture is based on taking God's Word seriously and applying it to every dimension of life. It's practical, timely, and relevant to all the issues of life, including how to keep focused on Jesus and the Resurrection during the Easter Season.

WHAT'S YOUR COMMUNICATION STYLE?

One of the biggest and most common problems families face today is a lack of healthy communication. It is an ever-increasing cause for frustration among kids and parents alike. Communication can be defined as the act of sharing or exchanging information. Clear, loving communication in your family is imperative for balanced living in a junk-food culture. What kind of sharing takes place in your home? Is the exchange of information one-sided in your family?

Dr. Lawrence Richards has provided a helpful explanation of parent-child communication. Drawing from the work of Ross Snyder, Richards characterizes four levels of parental response and communication through the following illustration.

A child in a boat is headed for certain disaster. He obviously made a bad decision upstream. His parent will respond in one of four ways.

1. The *advice-giver* is far removed from the emotional crisis. He hollers, "Row harder! Why did you get into the water in the first place? What a stupid kid! I told you not to do it. Didn't you read the warning signs?"

2. The *reassurer* is closer to the situation and responds, "You were a good kid. Your mother and I love you. Of the last three people who went over the falls, two survived. Good luck!"

3. The *understander* steps into the water and says, "Hey, the current is very strong here. You really are in trouble, aren't you? Let me see if I can get you some help."

4. The *self-revealer* gets into the boat with the child and immediately starts paddling to safety.[8]

In my book *The Seduction of Our Children*, Neil Anderson and I cited another example of parent-child communication.[9] Suppose your child comes home from school with sorrow written all over his face. You ask him what's wrong, and he tells you that his best friend has rejected him. How would you respond?

If you are an advice-giver you might say something like, "I never did like that kid anyway. What did you do to make him reject you? Next time be more careful about choosing your friends. I think what you need to do is . . . ."

If you are a reassurer you will probably wrap your arms around him and say, "Your mother and I love you. You're a good kid, and I know you will survive this crisis. You'll find another friend."

If you are an understander, you might respond, "Hey, that hurts doesn't it? Can we sit down and talk about it? Can you share with me what happened?"

But, if you're a self-revealer, you will give the child a hug and sit quietly with him for a moment reflecting on a time you were rejected. Then you may respond, "Two years ago my best friend turned his back on me. I trusted him as much as I trusted anyone. It was one of the most painful experiences of my life. I sense you are going through the same thing as I did."

We have asked hundreds of teenagers to identify how their parents respond to similar situations. Ninety-five percent identified their parents as advice-givers. Five percent said their parents were reassurers. Not one teenager identified their parents as understanders or self-revealers. I'm not saying that you don't need to give advice and offer reassurance to your child from time to time. Nor is any one particular response appropriate in every situation. But a serious communication problem exists when kids report that their parents respond almost exclusively with advice-giving and reassurance.

When your child is hurt or in trouble, he needs a self-revealer to get into the boat with him. If you don't adopt this communication style, your child may eventually be the victim of an even greater disaster. We should all strive to be the kind of parent a son or daughter can feel comfortable coming to and confiding in. If our kids know that we will respond to them with love, trust, and respect—no matter what they tell us—they will open up like flowers in the warm sun.

IMPROVE YOUR PARENTING STYLE

Make a commitment to establish a foundation for healthy communication in your family. As the parent, make sure you get involved in making this happen. Comedian Bill Cosby, in his book *Fatherhood*, said, "I've chosen to be involved in the raising of my children." As parents, we must make a commitment to be actively involved in every dimension of our children's lives. The more involved we become in the lives of our kids, the more time we must sacrifice. Just remember, it will always cost you something, whether you pay now or pay later. The difference is that if you wait until later, it's always more expensive.

When you start getting more involved in the life of your kids, you will learn not only what their likes and dislikes are but also to appreciate them. As our kids get older, they get busier, but that should not preclude us from being involved in their lives. Do you enjoy spending time with your kids and doing things that interest them? Have you developed a mutual interest in things you can do together?

On my son's last birthday I received one of the greatest compliments of my entire fathering experience. Typically we have had a combined birthday party for Tony and his twin sister Kati, but this time it was different. Kati wanted to have a slumber party with her girlfriends and go ice skating. Tony wanted to have some guys friends spend the night and then go tour the March Air Base Museum. My wife, Tami, volunteered to take the girls, and I happily agreed to take the guys. (Ice skating is not my thing; I usually end up spending more time crawling on the ice than skating!)

After spending several hours with Tony and the guys touring different parts of the museum, we went to a fast-food restaurant for a late lunch. It was fun sitting around the table interacting with these five young guys and learning about life from their perspective. Later that night at dinner, Tony told me that his friends thought I was "really cool." So I asked Tony what he thought of me. "I think you're cool too, Dad," was his response. I couldn't have asked for a better compliment. And what a great reminder about the importance of developing relationships with my kids. Spend time building relationships with your kids if you aren't already doing so. It's an important key to healthy communication, and the other benefits are awesome as well!

Now, let's take a look at some sound ideas for parenting in the twenty-first century. These ideas are foundational for understanding your kids and building healthy relationships with them. Be careful of glancing through as just doing a basic review of things isn't enough. The real issue is whether you are practicing these steps.

1. GET IN TOUCH WITH YOUR KIDS

All too frequently I find that parents know more about their ancestral family tree than they do about the current activities of their children. That's why an important element of parenting is getting a grasp on the likes, dislikes, and lifestyles of our kids. This can only happen when a conscious effort is made to invade their world and counter their culture. Without this hands-on knowledge, it's tough to earn the right to be heard or the respect of your children.

In our position as parents we can attempt to enforce the right to be heard, but it's not nearly as effective as earning it.

In 1 Corinthians 9:22 we find a truth that can be applied for this very element of parenting. "When I am with those whose consciences bother them easily, I don't act as though I know it all and don't say they are foolish; the result is that they are willing to let me help them. Yes, whatever a person is like, I try to find common ground with him so that he will let me tell him about Christ and let Christ save him" (TLB). The apostle Paul gives several important principles for parenting: Establish common ground with your kids and avoid a know-it-all attitude. Instead, learn from your kids about their world, letting them know that you accept them for who they are. Also, be sensitive to their needs and concerns. Most importantly, look for opportunities to live out and share your faith with your kids.

2. Learn to Listen

Once again the Bible provides us with some relevant advice on this aspect of parenting. Proverbs 18:13 says, "Answering before listening is both stupid and rude" (TM). Sometimes it's easy to advise or correct your child in a given situation before you have really heard with careful attention what he or she has to say. This takes time and effort, but it beats becoming like the person who is always saying, "Don't confuse me with the facts!"

Kids today need their parents to do more than just hear them out. They need moms and dads who will carefully listen to them. Webster's Dictionary defines listening as "to hear with thoughtful attention." Do you really listen to your kids? How about your spouse?

James 1:19 offers this additional advice in regards to listening: "Everyone should be quick to listen, slow to speak and slow to become angry." This verse is encouraging parents to put a mental stopwatch on their conversations and to keep track of how much they talk and how much they listen. Listening demonstrates to our kids that we really do care and think that what they have to say is important. Learning to listen can greatly improve parent-child relationships.

3. WORK AT UNDERSTANDING

Do you really comprehend the challenges your kids are facing in the twenty-first century—especially the older children? Forty percent of kids surveyed say that their views are either ignored or bypassed by parents. Consequently, they conclude that their parents don't really care about them or their opinions. Our ability to grasp their outlook about different issues in life enables us to better demonstrate our care and concern for them, as well as to provide proper guidance for facing the issues of life. Learning to understand them is foundational to building positive relationships with your children. At the core of understanding are two important concepts. First, as parents, we must become thoroughly familiar with the personality and disposition of each child. Secondly, we must work at putting ourselves in the position of our children and gain more insight about the world in which they live. When speaking to parents, I often comment, "I know you are aware that we live in a new millennium, but do you realize what that means in relationship to your kids?"

Things are remarkably different today than when we grew up. Certainly there are similar problems, as with previous generations, such as drug and alcohol abuse, premarital sex, and rebellion, to name a few. However, the problems facing kids today are more complex, and the intensity is far greater than for any previous generation. That's why it is important for parents today to put themselves in their children's place. A lot of the strain between parents and kids nowadays could be reduced through better communication and understanding. It's been said that home is not where you live but where they understand you.

Proverbs 11:12 reminds us that "a person of understanding holds their tongue." How many times have you said something that you regret right after the words rolled past your lips? Imagine how different family life might be if we as parents worked harder at understanding our children and their perspective before we spoke. Earlier in this chapter we talked about the importance of earning the right to be heard. According to Proverbs 13:15, "good understanding wins favor." Gaining favor through understanding can help us navigate through a multitude of childrearing issues.

4. Be a Source of Encouragement

Let's face it, we all need encouragement. But this is especially true of kids today. Our world is not a very encouraging place to live. Despair, resentment, and disillusionment enshroud this generation. That's why it is so important for our homes to be places of hope and help. Kids need a safe refuge where they are sure someone cares and wants the best for them.

Encouragement is an important principle woven throughout the New Testament. Look at 1 Thessalonians 5:11: "Therefore encourage one another and build each other up, just as in fact you are doing." Life is a long-distance marathon race. There are times when your feet ache, your throat burns, and your whole body cries out for you to stop. This is when you need to have supporters, people who believe in you. Their encouragement helps to push you along and motivates you to hang in there. Christians are to encourage one another in the same way. This is especially true for parents and their children. A word of encouragement offered at just the right time can be the difference between continuing to run the race of life and collapsing along the way. Look around your home. Be sensitive to the need for encouragement that other family members may have; offer supportive words or actions.

5. Love Them Genuinely

Everyone believes love is important, but we usually think of it as a feeling. In reality, genuine love is a choice and an action. First Corinthians 13:4–7 puts it this way: "Love is very patient and kind, never jealous or envious, never boastful or proud, never haughty or selfish or rude. Love does not demand its own way. It is not irritable or touchy. It does not hold grudges and will hardly even notice when others do it wrong. It is never glad about injustice, but rejoices whenever truth wins out. If you love someone you will be loyal to him no matter what the cost. You will always believe in him, always expect the best of him, and always stand your ground in defending him" (TLB).

These verses offer a great checklist to examine the kind of love we demonstrate toward members of our family. Our kids especially need this kind of love if they are going to survive in a junk-food culture. However, the kind of love the Bible is talking about is not humanly possible without help. God is the source of our love; he loved us enough to sacrifice his only Son for us, taking the punishment for our sins. Jesus is the ultimate example of what it means to love. Everything he did in life and death was supremely loving. The Holy Spirit gives us the power to love. God's love always involves a choice and an action, and our love for our children should be just like his.

6. Be an Example

Kids today need role models—examples for how to deal with the issues of life. They are looking for people who will lead the way and demonstrate to them how to make sense out of life. By far the best place for them to learn this is in the home. However, kids are also quick to pick up on hypocrisy, especially with Mom and Dad. How many times have you told your child not to say or do something only to hear them respond, "But you do it, why can't I?"

I saw this classically illustrated while speaking at a series of meetings at a church in northern California. At that time I used to do a seminar for kids entitled, "How Is Rock Music Changing Your Life?" Right after speaking in the Sunday morning service at this church, a couple came up to talk with me. "Reverend Russo," they said with a slight southern drawl, "we're so glad you're gonna speak about the evils of that rock music to the young people this afternoon." "Gee, thanks folks," I replied. "By the way, just out of curiosity, what kind of music do you listen to?" They both straightened up, grinned at each other, and said, "Why, we listen to American music." "What kind of music might that be?" I asked, fully knowing how they would respond. "We like to think of it as

God's music—country-western music." I didn't have the heart to tell them that part of my presentation that afternoon would cover country music. When you get right down to it, the lyrics and the lifestyles exalted in country music are just as bad as rock music. And you can understand the lyrics better because the music isn't as loud!

Here was a prime example of the hypocrisy that our kids experience so many times each day. Adults criticize their music, then turn right around and listen to something or watch a video that is just as bad or even worse. Let's be careful to avoid the "Do as I say, not as I do" syndrome. Matthew 7:5 puts it this way: "Hypocrite! First get rid of the log from your own eye; then perhaps you will see well enough to deal with the speck in your friend's eye" (NLT). God doesn't expect us to be perfect, but our kids expect us to be real. Strive to live a life that reflects responsibility and accountability. Be an example.

THE BOTTOM LINE

Parenting is never easy. It takes time, energy, and effort. In the last twenty years we've seen increased spending on education and social welfare, parents who are better educated, families that are smaller—and yet our children are at greater risk than ever before. Why? A major contributing factor is a generation of parents who are unwilling to spend time building values into the lives of their children. There is no substitute for sharing our lives with our kids. A simple way to stay in touch with your kids and spend time with them is to make sure that you have at least one meal per day as a family. Sit together around the table and make sure that the television set is off. Mealtime can be a great opportunity to connect as a family and to find out about each member's activities for the day. The concept of having a meal together may be new to your family, but it is definitely worth making a priority in your home.

Ultimately, if we want our children to survive in this junk-food culture, we must not only spend time building values into their lives, we must also help them develop a vital, personal relationship with the Jesus of Easter. He is our strength, hope, and peace in a confused world that has lost its way. Don't assume that your child is a Christian simply because you are a Christian and have taken him to Sunday school on a regular basis. He must personally receive Jesus Christ as Savior and Lord, and who better to lead them in making that commitment than you, his parents? Here are a few important guidelines for leading your child to Christ.

Pray for your child's salvation. You can't argue your child into becoming a Christian, but you can pray for him and allow God to prepare his heart to receive the gospel. Your child's salvation should be at the top of your prayer list.

Tell stories. Kids often understand concepts better when they are presented through stories. Tell or read your child Bible stories about people who were challenged to surrender their lives to Christ. For example, you might consider using one of the following: Jesus talking with Nicodemus (John 3), or Jesus and Zacchaeus (Luke 19). Also, expose your child to good Christian children's books that present God's love and plan of salvation.

Give a simple gospel presentation. At some point you must clearly and lovingly share the gospel with your child and invite him to receive Christ. There are many excellent tracts available that summarize the gospel in terms a child can understand. Whether you use one of these tools or not, your presentation should include the following basic truths:

- God loves you and wants to give you peace, eternal and abundant life (John 3:16; 10:10; Rom. 5:1).
- You are sinful and separated from God (Rom. 3:23; 6:23).
- Jesus paid the penalty for your sin when he died on the cross (John 14:6; Rom. 5:8).
- You must confess your sin and receive Jesus Christ as Savior and Lord (John 1:12; 1 John 1:9; Rev. 3:20).

As you talk with your child about spiritual matters, be sure to speak at their level. Don't use "Christianese" or abstract theological terms ("saved," "repent," "justification," etc.) without thoroughly explaining their meaning in words your child can understand. Also, don't try to scare or manipulate your child into making a response. Simply present the gospel, answer their questions, and allow the Holy Spirit to bring them to the point of deciding to receive Christ.

Give a clear invitation. After you have explained the plan of salvation and are convinced that your child understands it, say something like, "Would you like to receive Jesus right now?" If they respond negatively, accept their decision. Continue praying for them and keep on sharing the gospel with them in the future. If they say yes, lead them in a simple prayer by having them read it aloud or repeat it after you phrase by phrase. You can use the following prayer:

Dear Jesus,

Thank you for loving me. I believe you died for me on the cross. I am sorry for my sins. I ask you to give me a new life and make me a part of God's family. Please help me to love and obey you.

In Jesus' name, amen.

Review their decision. After leading your child in a prayer of salvation, take a few minutes to talk through the following questions to help them understand what has just happened:

- What did you just do? say?
- What did Jesus do when you opened your heart to him? (Rev. 3:20)
- What did you become when you received Jesus into your heart? (John 1:12)
- Where is Jesus right now?

If you or your child receive Christ as a result of this chapter, please contact our ministry using the information in the back of the book. We'd like to pray for you and send you some information on how to begin this new relationship with Jesus Christ.

CHAPTER 10

The Hope of Easter

Jeremy was born with a twisted body, a slow mind, and a chronic, terminal illness that was slowly killing him. His parents had tried to give him as normal a life as possible and sent him to St. Theresa's Elementary School.

At the age of twelve, Jeremy was only in second grade and seemingly unable to learn. His teacher, Miss Doris Miller, often became exasperated with him. He would squirm in his seat, drool, and make grunting noises. At other times he spoke clearly and distinctly, as if a small beam of light had penetrated the darkness of his brain. Most of the time, however, Jeremy irritated his teacher. One day she called his parents and asked them to come for a consultation. As his parents sat quietly in the empty classroom, she said to them, "Jeremy really belongs in a special school. It isn't fair to him to be with younger children who don't have learning problems. There's a five-year gap between his age and that of the other students!"

Jeremy's mother cried softly while her husband spoke. "Miss Miller," he said, "there is no school of that kind nearby. It would be a terrible shock for Jeremy if we had to take him out of this school. We know he really likes it here." Miss Miller sat for a long time after they left, staring at the snow outside the window. Its coldness seemed to seep into her soul. She wanted to sympathize with them. After all, their only child had a terminal illness. But it wasn't fair to keep him in her class. She had eighteen other children to teach, and Jeremy was a terrible distraction. Furthermore, he would never learn to read or write. Why waste any more time trying?

As she pondered the situation, guilt washed over her. "Oh God," she said aloud, "here I am complaining when my problems are nothing compared with that poor family's! Please help me to be more patient with Jeremy." From that day on, she tried hard to ignore Jeremy's noises, squirming, and blank stares. One day he limped up to her desk, dragging his bad leg behind him. "I love you, Miss Miller," he exclaimed loudly enough for the whole class to hear. The other children snickered, and her face turned bright red. She stammered, "Wh-Why, that's very nice, Jeremy. Now please take your seat."

Spring came and the children talked excitedly about the coming of Easter. Miss Miller told them the story of Jesus, and then to emphasize the idea of new life springing forth, she gave each of the children a large plastic egg. "Now," she said to them, "I want you to take this home and bring it back tomorrow with something inside that shows new life. Do you understand?"

"Yes, Miss Miller!" the children responded enthusiastically, all except for Jeremy. He just listened intently, and his eyes never left her face. He didn't even make his usual noises. Had he understood what she had said about Jesus' death and resurrection? Did he understand the assignment? Perhaps she should call his parents and explain the project to them.

That evening, Doris' kitchen sink stopped up. She called the landlord and waited an hour for him to come by and unclog it. After that, she still had to shop for groceries, iron a blouse, and prepare a vocabulary test for the next day. She completely forgot about phoning Jeremy's parents. The next morning, nineteen children came to class, all laughing and talking as they placed their eggs in the large wicker basket on Miss Miller's desk.

After they completed their math lesson, it was time to open the eggs. In the first egg, Miss Miller found a flower. "Oh, yes, a flower is certainly a sign of new life," she said. "When plants peek through the ground, we know that spring is here." A small girl in the first row waved her arms. "That's my egg, Miss Miller," she called out. The next egg contained a plastic butterfly that looked very real. Doris held it up. "We all know that a caterpillar changes and turns into a beautiful butterfly. Yes, that's new life too." Little Judy smiled proudly and said, "Miss Miller, that one is mine." Next Miss Miller found a rock with moss on it. She explained that the moss also showed life. Billy spoke up from the back of the classroom. "My Daddy helped me!"

Then she opened the fourth egg. She gasped. The egg was empty! Surely it must be Jeremy's, she thought. He had obviously not understood her instructions. If only she had not forgotten to phone his parents. Not wanting to embarrass him, she quietly set the egg aside and reached for another. Suddenly Jeremy spoke up. "Miss Miller, aren't you going to talk about my egg?" Flustered, Doris replied, "But Jeremy, your egg is empty!" He looked into her eyes and said softly, "Yes, but Jesus' tomb was empty too!" Miss Miller was stunned. When she could finally speak again, she asked him, "Do you know why the tomb was empty?"

"Oh yes!" Jeremy exclaimed. "Jesus was killed and put in there. Then his Father raised him up!" Just then the recess bell rang. While the children excitedly ran out to the schoolyard, Doris cried. The ice inside her seemed to melt away.

Three months later Jeremy died. Those who paid their respects at the mortuary were surprised to see nineteen eggs on top of his casket, every one of them empty.[10]

Jeremy understood what new life was all about, even better than his teacher. In spite of learning disabilities, he was able to grasp the important spiritual truth that the empty tomb symbolized. What does the empty tomb represent to you? Life? Hope?

People everywhere today are asking where the hope is. They are feeling discouraged and powerless at the decay all around them. Broken hearts and lives are on every side, afflicting both young and old. They are searching for a ray of hope to give them the courage to keep on living.

Fifteen-year-old Melissa was like this. I met her after speaking at an assembly at her high school in North Carolina. She stood patiently in line with the other kids, waiting to talk with me. "Can we talk privately for a minute?" she asked. "Sure," I said. "Let's just step over here."

"Thanks for saving my life," she said. "Things have been really bad in my life lately. Too much pain, too many problems. I just couldn't take any more. So last night I had made up my mind to kill myself. I was going to take care of it today. Your message in the assembly gave me hope, a reason to live. Thanks a lot, Steve."

As Melissa walked away, arm in arm with a couple of other girlfriends, I knew why I had come to speak in North Carolina that week. If just for this one young life, it was worth it. Unfortunately, Melissa's story is all too common.

Everywhere I travel I meet people just like her who cannot handle the pain and the issues of life. It's no wonder; just look around—the breakdown of the family, disease and AIDS, gangs, violence, the environment, and the list goes on and on. There is little encouraging news, be it social or political, in the newspapers.

Hopelessness has reached new proportions, and the effects are devastating. People will do almost anything when there is a hopeless future. Even popular music today reflects the feelings of hopelessness in our world. It discusses all the issues but offers only a temporary escape, without any lasting answers.

Where do we find hope that will last and enable us to cope with the challenges of life in the twenty-first century? There is only one place.

THE SOURCE FOR HOPE

The apostle Peter wrote his letter to the early Christians who were struggling under the pressures and adversities of life. "Praise be to the God and Father of our Lord Jesus Christ! In his great mercy he has given us new birth into a living hope through the resurrection of Jesus Christ from the dead" (1 Pet. 1:3). There is hope, and we obtain it when we become part of God's family. Peter's words offer hope in difficult times. He bases this confidence on what God has done on our behalf through Jesus Christ. Notice that this hope is "living." We have a living hope because of the blood Christ shed on the cross for our sins and because he conquered death through his resurrection. This hope is not only for the future and eternal life. It begins the moment we receive Christ, and it affects every dimension of our lives here on earth.

God's Word is filled with promises of hope for those who become part of his forever family. Consider these promises:

- "There is surely a future hope for you, and your hope will not be cut off" (Prov. 23:18).
- "For I know the plans I have for you," says the Lord. "They are plans for good and not for disaster, to give you a future and a hope" (Jer. 29:11 NLT).

Stop for a moment to meditate on and pray about these two promises. Read them over again. Ask God, in prayer, what this means to you personally. How can you apply this truth to your life? Too often we gloss over powerful, life-changing truths like these without taking time to digest and apply them. If you are going through a difficult time in your life, you may want to revisit these verses frequently each day as source of encouragement. You may even want to memorize them, giving yourself access to these truths continually throughout the day.

Remember, God knows the future, and his plans for us are good and full of hope. We are not here by accident; he has a purpose for our lives and a destiny for us to fulfill. That's why it is so important for us to follow God's future plan for our lives rather than our own misguided ideas. The benefit to us of this act of obedience will be immeasurable hope. This does not mean our lives will be free from adversity, pain, or suffering—that's all part of life. Jesus promised us that we would have trouble in this life: "I have told you all this so that you may have peace in me. Here on earth you will have many trials and sorrows. But take heart, because I have overcome the world" (John 16:33 NLT). However we are not alone, we have a living God to see us through to a positive conclusion. Ultimate victory has already been won!

Hope comes from God, and ours is secured by the resurrection of Jesus Christ.

THE EFFECTS OF HOPE

Biblical hope is motivational and encouraging. It produces many things, including confidence in God. "And we know that God causes everything to work together for the good of those who love God and are called according to his purpose for them" (Rom. 8:28 NLT). Even though evil is prevalent in our world, God is able to turn it around for our ultimate good. But remember, this promise is not for everyone. It's only for those who love God and walk on his pathway for life.

Hope gives us endurance in times of tribulation. "Not only so, but we also rejoice in our sufferings, because we know that suffering produces perseverance; perseverance, character; and character, hope" (Rom. 5:3–4). Hope grows as we learn all that God has planned for us. Difficulties will also help us to grow. Problems we encounter will develop our endurance. God will give us the ability to stand strong under tremendous weight and pressure without collapsing. The growth process continues as our character is strengthened and our trust in God is deepened, which gives us confidence for the future.

Ultimately, hope brings a sense of stability to our lives. In Hebrews 6:18–19 we read, "God did this so that, by two unchangeable things in which it is impossible for God to lie, we who have fled to take hold of the hope offered to us may be greatly encouraged. We have this hope as an anchor for the soul, firm and secure." In ancient times, cities of refuge were provided for those who sought protection from avengers for an accidental killing (see Num. 35 or Deut. 19). Christ is a refuge that we can run to today. Not only has he paid the penalty for our sin; he also offers protection from destruction in life's disasters. And like a supernatural anchor, hope in Christ gives us courage in the storms of life. God's hope keeps us secure in times of trouble and turmoil.

OUR ENDLESS HOPE

Where would you be this Easter without Jesus? How different would your life be having not experienced the hope that only God can offer?

As Christians we have good news to offer to the world, news that brings hope. This makes our message unique. This is why we must keep this message alive at all costs.

God raised Jesus from the grave after three days not only to prove that he had power over sin and death but also to give us a guarantee of hope and new life. The Resurrection was the most unique moment in history. After that first Easter morning the world was never the same. Ahead of Jesus was eternal life; behind him death lay in a heap of linen. Jesus is not only the reason for our hope, he is our *only* hope. Only he can rescue us. Where have you placed your hope?

Maybe you have never responded to God's love as demonstrated by Christ's death on the cross. If you have never come to God and asked for forgiveness, this hope is not yet yours. But if you come to the place in your life where you recognize that you can't make it on your own, why not take a few minutes right now and follow the "Steps to Peace with God"[11] listed below. Then pray the simple prayers suggested. Receiving Christ is the most important thing you will ever do in life. There's no greater joy than knowing God personally. Once you've made the decision to follow Jesus, Easter takes on a whole new meaning.

STEPS TO PEACE WITH GOD

1. GOD'S PURPOSE: PEACE AND LIFE

God loves you and wants you to experience peace and life—abundant and eternal.

"We have peace with God through our Lord Jesus Christ." Romans 5:1

"For God so loved the world that he gave his one and only Son, that whoever believes in him shall not perish but have eternal life." John 3:16

Why don't most people have this peace and abundant life that God planned for us to have?

2. THE PROBLEM: OUR SEPARATION

God created us in his own image to have an abundant life. He did not make us as robots to automatically love and obey him.

God gave us a will and freedom of choice. We chose to disobey God and go our own willful way. We still make this choice today. This results in separation from God.

"For all have sinned and fall short of the glory of God." Romans 3:23

"For the wages of sin is death, but the gift of God is eternal life in Christ Jesus our Lord." Romans 6:23

Our choice results in separation from God.

People have tried in many ways to bridge this gap between themselves and God. Our attempts to reach God include good works, religion, philosophy, and morality . . . .

"There is a way that seems right to a man, but in the end it leads to death." Proverbs 14:12

"But your iniquities have separated you from your God; your sins have hidden his face from you, so that he will not hear." Isaiah 59:2

No bridge reaches God . . . except one.

3. GOD'S BRIDGE: THE CROSS

Jesus Christ died on the cross and rose from the grave. He paid the penalty for our sin and bridged the gap between God and people.

"For there is one God and one mediator between God and men, the man Christ Jesus." 1 Timothy 2:5

"For Christ died for sins once for all, the righteous for the unrighteous, to bring you to God." 1 Peter 3:18

"But God demonstrates his own love for us in this: While we were still sinners, Christ died for us." Romans 5:8

God has provided the only way and each person must make a choice. . . .

4. OUR RESPONSE: RECEIVE CHRIST

We must trust Jesus Christ as Lord and Savior and receive him by personal invitation.

"Here I am! I stand at the door and knock. If anyone hears my voice and opens the door, I will come in and eat with him, and he with me." Revelation 3:20

"Yet to all who received him, to those who believed in his name, he gave the right to become children of God." John 1:12

"That if you confess with your mouth, 'Jesus is Lord,' and believe in your heart that God raised him from the dead, you will be saved." Romans 10:9

Here is how you can receive Christ:

1. Admit your need (I am a sinner).

2. Be willing to turn from your sins (repent).

3. Believe that Jesus Christ died for you on the cross and rose from the grave.

4. Through prayer, invite Jesus Christ to come in and control your life through the Holy Spirit (Receive him as Lord and Savior).

How to Pray:

Dear Jesus,

I know that I have sinned and need your forgiveness. I now turn from my sins to follow you. I believe that you died on the cross to take the punishment for my sins and that you came back to life after three days. I invite you to come into my heart and life. I want you to be my Savior and Lord. Thank you for your love and the gift of eternal life.

In Jesus' name, amen.

If you prayed this prayer to receive Christ, please let us know by using the contact information in the back of this book. This is just the beginning of a great new life with Jesus. Not only do we want to pray for you; moreover, we also want to send you more information to help you grow and deepen in this new relationship with God.

CHAPTER 11

Now What?

Considering you've made it to this point in the book, one of two things must have transpired. Either you've finished this volume after diligently reading through it, or you've jumped ahead to look for an exciting conclusion! If you made the effort to faithfully read through each chapter, I would like you to take a few minutes for personal reflection and application.

It would be too easy to set this book on the shelf and move on. However, that wasn't my intent in writing it. My desire is that this material would motivate you to do something to practically apply the information to your own situation as a concerned parent or as someone wanting to celebrate Easter in a whole new way. To do this effectively will require some time on your part, but I believe it's worth every minute invested.

Take some time to review each chapter, using the brief outline and questions I have provided in this section of the book. With some chapters you will have received content that was more informative than practical. Regardless, take the time to reflect and apply anyway. In most cases I think you should be able to find at least one concept you can implement in your personal circumstances.

If you are married, you may want to discuss these thoughts with your spouse. If you are a parent, you'll doubtless want to discuss the material with your children. When it comes down to application, remember the phrase the Nike Corporation has made famous: "Just Do It." Invest a few moments in the study of Easter, and you'll find a rich reward as we celebrate the resurrection of our Savior, Jesus Christ.

DISCUSSION QUESTIONS

1. THE FIRST EASTER

- What surprised you the most about the history of Easter?
- Do you recognize any remnants from ancient pagan festivals in the way Easter is celebrated in your community?
- Take some time to think about what Easter meant that first year and what it means now.

2. SPECIAL DAYS AND CUSTOMS AT EASTER

- Have new insights into the history of Easter's special days and customs added significance to you individually and to your family's celebration of Easter?
- How important do you feel it is to incorporate new ethnic traditions into your family's Easter celebration?
- Do you have friends who celebrate differently, according to a different ethnic background? If so, could your two families celebrate together in order to share traditions?

3. EASTER AROUND THE WORLD

- What customs are practiced in the land of your ancestors?
- What are some fun things from your ethnic heritage that you could incorporate into your Easter celebration?

For Children

- Take time to look into your family's cultural heritage with your children. Ask them what they think would be fun to make part of your family's Easter holiday tradition.

4. EASTER EGGS, BUNNIES, AND JELLY BEANS

- What are some of your favorite symbols and foods at Easter? Why?
- Are there some new things that you read about in this chapter that you would like to adopt into your family's celebration? What are they and why do you want them to be a part of your Easter?

- Are you helping your children distinguish between fiction and fact?

5. THE GREAT EASTER DEBATE
- Go back and review the five "if" statements Paul listed in 1 Corinthians 15 in regards to the importance of the resurrection of Christ. Carefully examine the possibilities he poses. Approach each "if" logically. What do they mean to you and your faith in Christ?
- What is the most important aspect of Easter to you in light of the various positions debaters take in this chapter?
- If Christ had not died, what would it mean for Christians?

6. WHATEVER HAPPENED TO EASTER VACATION?
- What differences have you noticed, compared with when you were a child, in how our society observes Easter?
- What do you think Jesus would do with the Easter celebration in our society?

For Children
- What would Jesus want you to do on Easter?

7. CONFRONTING THE CROSS
- What cross do you carry? What have you found yourself doing to try and earn God's favor?
- Jesus had confidence and perfect peace as he placed his spirit in the Father's hands. Do you have enough peace and trust to place your life in the Father's hands?
- What dimension of your life do you need to surrender to God today?

8. GETTING BACK TO THE HEART OF EASTER
- Is Christ's death and resurrection at the center of your family's Easter traditions?
- Does your family know when to celebrate and when to reflect on the significance of Easter?
- What are you going to do differently this year during the Easter holiday season?

9. Parenting in a Junk-food Culture
- What are you doing to develop relationships with your kids?
- Do you pray with and for your children?
- What is your greatest struggle in parenting? What kind of help do you need to overcome this struggle?

10. The Hope of Easter
- Where have you placed your hope?
- How has the hope of Easter changed your life?
- Who do you need to share the hope of Easter with? Be specific: a relative, friend, or coworker? How and when do you plan to do this?

A FINAL WORD

As you continue to think about how you and your family will celebrate Easter, try to approach the issue with as biblical a viewpoint as possible. Keep in mind that just because there are pagan elements in the early history of Easter does not mean that it automatically disqualifies a Christian from participating in some modern-day form of those elements.

Also keep in mind that many American holidays, customs, and traditions have pagan remnants in their history. It would be pretty tough to say that participating in these holidays is wrong simply because of early pagan associations. Easter is, in fact, an example of a holiday that was derived from a pagan celebration. It is interesting to note that throughout history the church has appropriated these rituals and others and made them "Christian."

Even though the remnants of ancient paganism still endure, the practices and anti-Christian beliefs once associated with Easter and other holiday customs have long since disappeared. Who would dream of not using their monthly planner because the name origins of the days of the week were originally derived from pagan gods? What would a birthday party be without a cake and candles? Can you imagine not celebrating our Lord's resurrection on Easter Sunday because of a fertility ritual? That would be crazy! So when it comes to some Easter traditions, the way in which they were originally used should not determine our attitude toward them today.

Our responsibility as Christians is twofold. First, we must make every effort to keep the resurrection of Jesus Christ central to our celebration of Easter. We must never lose sight of the fact that Easter is crucial to the Christian faith. Second, whatever we do on or around Easter should glorify God. We should not compromise biblical values in any way. A word of caution here: Remember that the values of Christians are not always Christian, biblically based values. Just because someone in your church celebrates Easter in a particular way does not make it right or wrong for you. Don't forget that certain Easter traditions—like the Easter bunny—fall into the gray area of Christian living and are not specifically forbidden in the Bible. Always be aware that there will be differing opinions in the church community on how a Christian should respond to the culture. And be careful as you exercise your Christian freedom regarding Easter traditions that you do not become a "stumbling block to others weaker in the faith" (1 Cor. 8:9).

Let's look for creative ways to tell others why we celebrate Easter. And let's do all we can to help as many people as possible experience the resurrecting power of God in their lives this year!

Notes

1. *Draper's Book of Quotations for the Christian World,* Edythe Draper, compiler (Wheaton, Ill.: Tyndale House Publishers, Inc., 1992), 533.

2. Barbara Kantrowitz and Daniel McGinn, "When Teachers Are Cheaters," *Newsweek,* 19 June 2000, 48–49.

3. George Barna, "Living a Distinctly Christian Life," *Decision,* May 2000, 7.

4. Ibid.

5. This story was E-mailed to me; the author is unknown.

6. Geoffrey Cowley and Sharon Begley, "Fat for Life?" *Newsweek,* 3 July 2000, 43.

7. Bill Keane, "Family Circus," Bill Keane, Inc., 31 March 1999.

8. Lawrence O. Richards, *Youth Ministry* (Grand Rapids, Mich.: Zondervan, 1972), 139–45.

9. Neil Anderson and Steve Russo, *The Seduction of Our Children* (Eugene, Ore.: Harvest House, 1991), 148.

10. This story was E-mailed to me; the author is unknown.

11. "Steps to Peace with God," used with permission from the Billy Graham Evangelistic Association.

GLOSSARY:

Easter Terms and Definitions

Ascension. The Christian belief that Jesus Christ departed from the earth forty days after his resurrection. Christ was lifted up and taken out of sight on a cloud in the presence of the apostles (see Mark 16:19–20; Luke 24:50–51; Acts 1:1–14).

Atonement. The death of Christ on the cross as a redemptive sacrifice for our sins.

Christ. Son of God; Messiah; Anointed One.

Christian. One belonging to Christ, a believer in the faith.

Church calendar. Also referred to as the liturgical or ecclesiastical calendar. This is the methodical correlation of recurrent religious observances—feasts, festivals, and fasts. Time measures like the day, lunar month, solar year, and the seasons are used to help create the calendar.

Gospel. The message, or the "Good News," that Christ and his apostles announced.

Holy Week. This is the last week of the Lenten season. It begins with Palm Sunday and ends with Easter Sunday.

Incarnation. The word means "in flesh" and denotes the eternal Son of God taking on another nature through the virgin birth—humanity. The act of the preexistent Son of God voluntarily assuming a human body and human nature.

Jesus. The name given to God's Incarnate Son. It is the Greek form of "Jeshua" or "Joshua," meaning "the Lord is salvation" or "the salvation of the Lord."

Joseph of Arimathea. An honored member of the Jewish supreme court and a secret disciple of Jesus.

Justification. The lawful action that God as Judge takes to declare the believing sinner righteous.

Lent (Lenten season). Covers a forty-day period of prayer and fasting that begins on Ash Wednesday and ends with Easter. In the Eastern Church, Lent covers a seven-week period of time because it excludes both Saturdays and Sundays. The Western Church observance only lasts six and a half weeks because only Sundays are excluded. This season is set aside as a period of penance in preparation for the most important festival of the church calendar: Easter.

Litany. A prayer or series of petitions recited by a leader and congregation.

Liturgy. A public or state duty, priestly service.

Passover. An important feast in the Jewish calendar. The eight-day celebration commemorates the exodus of the Hebrews from Egypt and their safe retreat across the Red Sea. The name of this important Jewish festival (*pesach*, Hebrew for "passing over" or "protection") comes from instructions God gave to Moses in Exodus 12. In order to motivate Pharaoh to allow the Hebrews to leave Egypt, God was going to kill all the firstborn animals and people in the nation. In order to protect themselves, the Hebrews were instructed to mark their dwellings with lamb's blood so that God could identify them and pass over.

Pontius Pilate. The Roman governor of Judea at the time when Jesus was crucified.

Prophecy. The written or spoken word of God, forthtelling (corrective or comforting information) and foretelling (predictive information).

Prophet. One who forthtells corrective and comforting information or foretells predictive information.

Propitiation. The turning away of wrath by an offering. The death of Christ satisfied the wrath of God for man's sins.

Reconciliation. A change of relationship from hostility to harmony and peace between two parties. As a result of the death of Christ on the cross, reconciliation between God and man occurs.

Redemption. The liberation because of a payment made. For Christians, the payment made was the death of Christ.

Resurrection. The "standing up of a corpse" from the original Greek *anastasis nekron.* The resurrection of Jesus Christ is the center of the Christian faith. His resurrection established Jesus as the Son of God.

Sanhedrin. The ruling body of clergy in Judaism that controlled religious and political life.

Septuagint. A Greek translation of the Old Testament made in the third century B.C.

Sepulcher. Another name for the tomb in which Christ's body was placed after his death on the cross.

Talmud. A collection of Jewish writings of the early Christian centuries. There are two Talmuds: the Palestinian one and a later, more authoritative Babylonian one.

Tiberius. Tiberius Julius Caesar Augustus was the second Roman emperor following the death of Augustus. He was the reigning emperor at the time of the death of Christ.

Unleavened bread. Bread that was made without using any fermented dough. It was eaten at the Passover feast.

Upper room or upper chamber. A room that was frequently built on the roofs of houses and used in the summer time because it was cooler than the regular living quarters. One of these rooms was the scene of the Lord's Last Supper.

Via Dolorosa ("the sorrowful way"). The traditional route that Jesus traveled on the day of his crucifixion, from his audience before Pilot to Mount Calvary.

Vinegar. In today's culture it is a sour fluid obtained from the fermenting of cider. In biblical times, it came from wine. When Jesus was on the cross, he was offered wine mixed with gall or myrrh, but he refused it. Later Jesus was offered a mixture of water and vinegar on a sponge; this time he took it. This was a popular drink among the poor and Roman soldiers when they were in camp.

Watch. A man or group of men set to guard a city, situation, or people. There was a Roman watch (group of soldiers) that was assigned to guard the tomb of Jesus.

Suggested Reading

Christ in Easter: A Family Celebration of Holy Week
Charles Colson, Billy Graham, Max Lucado, Joni Eareckson Tada
NavPress, Colorado Springs, Colo., 1990

Easter Bunny, Are You for Real?
Harold Myra
Thomas Nelson Publishers, Nashville, Tenn., 1979

Family Celebrations at Easter
Ann Hibbard
Baker Books, Grand Rapids, Mich., 1994

MINISTRY INFORMATION

For information on how to purchase audio and videotape resources and other books by Steve Russo, as well as information on the *Real Answers* radio program, newsletter, fact sheets, conferences, public school assemblies, and evangelistic crusades, contact:

Real Answers with Steve Russo
P. O. Box 1549
Ontario, California 91762

(909) 466-7060
Fax (909) 466-7056
E-mail: Russoteam@realanswers.com

You can also visit our website at:
www.realanswers.com